MW01680361

VOM Books
The publishing division of
The Voice of the Martyrs
Serving persecuted Christians since 1967
vom.org

BE INSPIRED BY THEIR STORIES

HEROIC FAITH

VOM BOOKS
The Voice of the Martyrs

Heroic Faith

VOM Books
A division of The Voice of the Martyrs
1815 SE Bison Road
Bartlesville, OK 74006

Lead Writer and Development Editor: Marti Pieper
Edited by: Sheryl Martin Hash
Interior Layout by: Greg Jackson

Softcover Edition: 978-0-88264-429-5
eBook: 978-0-88264-430-1
Audiobook: 978-0-88264-431-8

Library of Congress Control Number: 2025935028

Printed in the USA

CPC 24122

CONTENTS

THREE WAYS TO USE *HEROIC FAITH* RESOURCES WITH YOUR FAMILY, CLASS OR GROUP, AND CHURCH

1. **Scan the QR Code** and "Press Play and Pray" on the *Heroic Faith* videos. Viewers will be inspired by the faith of our persecuted Christian brothers and sisters and challenged toward a more heroic faith themselves.

Scan QR Code or browse to
vom.org/HeroicFaith

HEROIC FAITH

2. **Read *Heroic Faith*** and be inspired by additional stories and biblical insights into the heroic faith of persecuted Christians. Questions for individual reflection and family or group discussion are included at the end of each chapter.

3. **Bonus Material**: Visit vom.org/HeroicFaith to download additional *Heroic Faith* videos and questions for reflection and discussion for use with your family, class or group, and church.

"There is no law that obliges Christians to be dull, lukewarm, half-hearted. Christianity can be heroic."

—Richard Wurmbrand

INTRODUCTION

Heroes capture our attention. We admire the person who runs into a burning building to save the life of a stranger. We respect those who risk their lives to serve their country in the military. They selflessly put themselves in harm's way. They willingly pay a price they don't have to pay—a price they choose to pay. Often, those who chose to pay that price shy away from being called a hero, but their actions are unquestionably heroic.

"Heroic faith" is not a new descriptor for biblical disciples. For more than two thousand years, heroes of the faith have endured terrible suffering as they dedicate their lives to Jesus Christ. They choose to obey the Lord daily in order to advance Christ and his kingdom at any cost.

The eleventh chapter of Hebrews gives us a look at those with heroic faith, including Noah, Abraham and Sarah, Moses, Rahab, Gideon, Samuel, and David. The writer of Hebrews calls attention to the heroic faith of those

- » who through faith conquered kingdoms
- » who shut the mouths of lions
- » who quenched the fury of the flames
- » who escaped the edge of the sword
- » whose weakness was turned to strength
- » women who received back their dead, raised to life again
- » who were tortured and refused to be released

» who faced jeers and flogging
» who were chained and put in prison
» who were destitute and mistreated—those of whom the world was not worthy.

While there is ultimately only one true hero of our faith—Jesus Christ our Lord—biblical disciples cannot help but read the descriptions of the saints of old in Hebrews 11 and be inspired by their examples of biblical faith. Their God-centered lives run counter to the fleshly, temporal pull of self-centered existence that must be put to death daily.

While we long for that type of heroic faith ourselves, our insecurities may cause us to think it is something we could never achieve. But every person listed in Hebrews 11 was just like us—ordinary people developing a more heroic faith over a lifetime of trusting God and walking in obedience.

What do biblical disciples, who possess a *heroic faith*, value and live out? How can our faith be *more heroic*? As you examine your life, what characteristics might indicate your faith is heroic?

In *Heroic Faith*, you will meet and be inspired by biblical disciples who exemplify the foundation and the fruit of a heroic faith. They see with an eternal perspective, depend upon God alone, trust God's Word, and live a sacrificial life. That foundation of heroic faith then bears obvious fruit that embraces courage, faithful endurance, unwavering obedience, and steadfast love.

As you read the stories of these persecuted Christian brothers and sisters and realize that we are knit together—united by the blood and lordship of Christ—may you be inspired by how they live with heroic faith.

To help you develop a more heroic faith, we have included questions for reflection and discussion at the end of each chapter and free access to accompanying short feature films. As you learn from the examples found in God's Word and from members of the global body of Christ, we pray you will ask the Lord to examine your own heart and life, and walk with determination toward a more heroic faith.

The Voice of the Martyrs

CHAPTER 1

SEE WITH ETERNAL PERSPECTIVE

"The prayers of the widows themselves are for the Aucas. We look forward to the day when [they] will join us in Christian praise."

—Elisabeth Elliot[1]

No one would have blamed them for leaving. They had been traumatized by the brutal murders of their loved ones, brothers in Christ, and co-laborers in a remote jungle in Ecuador. Why would they stay?

Headlines carried the news worldwide when the Ecuador Five, as they came to be known, gave the ultimate sacrifice for the advancement of the gospel. Jim Elliot, Pete Fleming, Ed McCully, Nate Saint, and Roger Youderian were speared to death on January 8, 1956, by members of the Auca tribe (later known as the Waodani or Waorani), the very people they sought to reach. Only the day before, the five young missionaries initially met with members of the tribe, who had seemed friendly. Yet the Aucas retaliated the next day.

Less than three years after the tragedy, Jim Elliot's widow, Elisabeth, and her young daughter, Valerie, along with Nate Saint's sister Rachel, embraced a risky opportunity that God provided to live among the Auca people. Their acceptance of the challenge came only after many hours of prayer—and ultimately, forgiveness, grace, and understanding, as well as a more informed perspective.

"The Auca was trying to preserve his own way of life, his own liberty," Elisabeth Elliot wrote about her understanding of the Aucas' actions to kill the missionaries. "He believed the foreigners were a threat to that liberty, so he feels he had every right to kill them. In America, we decorate a man for defending his country."[2]

But what could motivate Elizabeth, who was still serving in Quito, Ecuador, to return to the place and to the people responsible for her husband's death? Both Rachel Saint and Elisabeth Elliot possessed a perspective aligned more with the eternal than the temporal. In fact, Elisabeth's biographer writes:

> It was not "admirable missionary zeal" that spurred her, nor desire. . . . She had felt then that she didn't care if she ever went to the Waodani or ever heard their name again.
>
> It was something beyond duty or misty-eyed missionary visions that spurred Betty straight toward the Waodani. "All I want is what You want," she wrote in a prayer in her journal. "I've sung it in tear-jerking missionary meetings, but I write it here with all of my heart—'Where He leads me, I will follow.'"[3]

Elisabeth, and the other women whose husbands perished at the hands of the Aucas, had never stopped praying for the salvation of the members of this people group. "The prayers of the widows themselves are for the Aucas. We look forward to the day when [they] will join us in Christian praise," she explained in *Through Gates of Splendor*, her memoir about the journey.[4]

Rather than remain focused on the image of lifeless bodies on a rocky jungle beach, she and Rachel saw what could be: a people claimed for Christ and his glory, added to the throng of nations worshiping around his throne.

FRESH FOCUS

Scripture records the stories of many others who viewed the world through a unique lens, one that allowed them to glimpse not a present but a future reality. This perspective, rooted not in a clock or calendar but in the timeless depths of eternity, allowed them to see as God sees—viewing the world through the lens of faith for the not-yet-realized, a faith we could call *heroic.*

Those who possess heroic faith see the world with eyes that understand, accept, and pursue the passion and priority of God. We find people like this throughout the pages of Scripture, where the writer of Hebrews has assembled many of them for us in that book's eleventh chapter. In fact, the Hebrews 11 listing of champions of the faith begins with a clear reference to their eternal perspective, describing faith as "the assurance of things hoped for, the conviction of things not seen" (Hebrews 11:1).

Noah, whose story is summarized in Hebrews 11:7, viewed life through that different lens. Not only did he stand out amid the wickedness of his day, but he also persevered in following God's command to build an ark (Genesis 6:9–21). Rather than complain about the painful reality, he fixed his eyes on God's promised rescue.

Noah truly had eyes to see what had not yet happened. The perspective he gained moved him to act *immediately* in view of God's *not yet*—the Lord's promise of things to come. Think of the faith it must have taken for a man who lived far from any sea and had never seen a flood (and, according to some Bible scholars, had never even experienced rain), to build a boat large enough to hold his family and a pair of animals and birds from every species (Genesis 7:2–3).

As with those of heroic faith today, Noah's faith rested on his ability to see the not-yet-seen—which flowed from his deep relationship with God, described in Hebrews 11:7 as his "reverent fear." Scripture also refers to him as "a righteous man, blameless in his generation" who "walked with God" (Genesis 6:9). This relationship served as the foundation for his unwavering trust in God's warning of judgment and his promise to preserve Noah's family.

The wicked culture of the day and the seeming foolishness of his desert construction project allow modern readers to picture Noah's neighbors jeering as he worked.

His story brings to life Paul's explanation of the Christian life in 2 Corinthians 5:7, where he says believers "walk by faith, not by sight."

Noah's confidence was in the God who made the promise—a God whose nature and character he trusted. That assurance in God steeled his obedience in the face of ridicule from a faithless crowd. Noah's confident reality, seeing God as provider, was something others could not fathom.

Yet, it was more than simply seeing. That eternal perspective quickly stirred his heart and mind as he believed what God had promised him; he saw it as God described it. His faith-filled vision aligned his sight with God's power, allowing him to act on the truth of what he saw.

NEW PERSPECTIVE

"Sang-chul" saw a heroic faith demonstrated long before he embraced it. For years, the lies of North Korean propaganda held him captive.

Trapped in the darkness of spiritual bondage, he feared physical imprisonment and worse.

North Korean children are taught in primary school that all missionaries are to be viewed with suspicion, likening them to terrorists, and that they even might be dangerous.

Sang-chul ventured into Chinese territory one day while searching for mushrooms in a mountainous region. He met a kind stranger who volunteered to sell Sang-chul's harvest in a nearby Chinese village and return the money to help Sang-chul and his family survive. This stranger kept his word and brought back the full sale price of the harvest of mushrooms.

Sang-chul didn't know this kind stranger was actually a Christian. As the two continued to meet, Pastor Han revealed that his kindness was the result of his faith in Christ. That disclosure frightened Sang-chul.

But his new friend continued selling Sang-chul's mushrooms, returning each time to give him all the money collected.

One day, Pastor Han told Sang-chul that God is real, and there is hope for every person who believes in him. Sang-chul was amazed when he heard someone speak the name of God, for that was forbidden and considered an act of treason in North Korea.

Despite his fear, Sang-chul's gaze began to shift away from his circumstances, out of his spiritual darkness and toward the light of eternity. In time, he asked Pastor Han for a Bible. As he read it, Sang-chul experienced the same transforming power that believers throughout the centuries have received when they are rooted in the Word of God. Ignoring the risks to his own life, Sang-chul took the bold step of sharing his faith with family and friends. Even his wife, who at first opposed his relationship with the friendly pastor, came to follow Christ.

Later, the tragic news came: Pastor Han had been killed for his faith. The steadfast witness that brought life to more than a thousand people resulted in his death at the hands of North Korean assassins.

Sang-chul was inspired by the sacrifice of Pastor Han, both in life and in death, and hopes that his own sacrifice, when the day comes, will be worthwhile for others.

YOUR KINGDOM COME

Let's consider this for a moment. Is our way of seeing life and circumstances worth clinging to at all costs? Do we have such a clear perspective on the value of our everyday pursuits that we are willing to put them above all else?

Well-meaning people, even those who attend church regularly and live seemingly good lives, often miss God's best. The press of this world, the pull of Satan, and even the pursuit of good things turn us away from God and toward the world. This often results in our choosing to follow a way that leads to death. Like a mirage-borne vision of an oasis for a thirsty desert traveler, the quest for worldly pleasures such as wealth, status, influence, and possessions only end in soul-crushing sand.

Deep inside, we long for more—just like Sang-chul, trapped in the darkness of the lies his government told him. We find *more* only when we align our perspective with God's as he resets our hearts and our vision toward seeing as he sees. With that fresh perspective comes the understanding that the world in which we live has an expiration date; everything in it is fading away. Scripture tells us the end of our world lies ahead (Matthew 24:9–24). Heaven and earth will pass away (Matthew 24:35). When we die, judgment is certain (Hebrews 9:27).

A biblical perspective opens our eyes to see the kingdom of God in the midst of the mirage of this world; his kingdom becomes the standard by which we live our lives. Jesus made it clear: the kingdom of God—his rule and reign in all things—is not some far-off, heaven-only concept but has been fulfilled with his coming.

Jesus revealed this after his cousin John's arrest at the hands of Herod Antipas. Scripture says the Savior "entered Galilee, proclaiming the gospel of God, and saying, 'The time is fulfilled, and the kingdom of God is at hand; repent and believe in the gospel'" (Mark 1:14–15). He also taught his disciples to pray using these now-familiar but powerful words: "Your kingdom come, your will be done, on earth as it is in heaven" (Matthew 6:10).

Nuanced in the meaning of the original language is the truth that God's kingdom would one day arrive, as Jesus had proclaimed. But it also reveals that we can see and know his kingdom today if we have eyes to see it—eyes that view life with an eternal perspective. As we face circumstances, trials, and opportunities, we must allow God to reset our hearts and our eyes—and continually look for his kingdom.

"THE SWEETEST TIME OF MY LIFE"

No one else would have described it as sweet. Instead, those who faced what one brother in Iran endured because of his Christian witness might have expressed bitterness, even hatred, toward their tormentors. But Iman, a former Iranian Muslim who now follows Jesus Christ, saw things from a different viewpoint—the fresh vision that builds a heroic faith.

By the fourth year of his salvation, Iman had knelt and prayed with more than a thousand people as they repented of their sins and committed their lives to Jesus Christ.

How many of the believers you know lead hundreds of people a year to Christ? This question is not nearly as challenging as Iman's arrest, interrogation, and imprisonment—all for the crime of sharing his faith. But through the lens of that faith, he explained how, as part of a network of young Christian leaders who provided both training and accountability, he saw this dangerous time as a divine opportunity:

> When they arrested me for no reason, I just knew God was sending me to a place to witness. So, I didn't fight so they would take me to jail. They took me to the jail, and I saw two people who were bound because their crimes were very serious. When I came to those people, I told them, "God has sent me to save you."
>
> So by faith, I believe that those who are around me, God has sent for me to share the gospel. So I shared the gospel very briefly, just about in 15 minutes, and they knelt and prayed to repent and receive Christ.
>
> I had only those 15 minutes to share the gospel because after I shared the gospel, immediately after, the police came and said, "You have been very good, and you shouldn't be here. You are very kind to us, and we want to release you." They opened the door and said I could go.
>
> When they opened the door to release me, I hugged those two criminals and they were crying and hugging me really hard. So the warden of the police was like, "You have only known these people for 15 minutes, and they act like you are family!"[5]

Iman maintained his faith-filled perspective even when, once again, he was imprisoned for his gospel witness. Fearing sexual assault from the prison guards, he cried out to the God who held his trust.

"I learned to focus on the presence of Jesus," Iman explained. "I said, 'Whatever happens, it is worth it for what you did for me.' I learned what it means to wrestle with God because at that point I told God, 'Even if they rape me, I will not renounce you.'"[6]

Despite twenty-one days in solitary confinement—followed by a move to a larger prison and assignment to a cell filled with murderers, addicts, and mentally ill prisoners—Iman kept his eyes on his loving Father. He prayed for his captors, asking God's blessings on their lives, marriages, and families. Guards were soon sneaking extra food to him—and fellow prisoners were asking how he maintained his positive attitude.

Thus began Iman's prison ministry, which he called "the sweetest time of my life."[7] Locked in the dangerous cell for eight days, he saw twenty-four of his fellow prisoners come to Christ, two of them convicted murderers awaiting execution.

But what happened on the fifth day of those eight days in that cell was astonishing. Prison officials told Iman he could put up bail money and be released. Instead of rushing to free himself, he continued his ministry in prison for three more days—until the guards grew suspicious about his decision to stay.

"I believe that when God sends us to some place, he prepares and equips us for that place," Iman said. "I knew I had a mission in that prison."[8]

After his release, Iman submitted his monthly ministry report to his leaders. The account didn't mention arrest, twenty-one days of solitary confinement, or time in prison—just ministry work: "In the past month, I was able to share the gospel with one hundred people. Of those, twenty-four prayed for the forgiveness of sins and committed their lives to following Jesus Christ."[9]

Several weeks passed before his leaders realized the truth—Iman's ministry that month took place inside a prison.

"The day I was out of jail, I continued my ministry," he said. "Until my last breath, I owe Jesus. Whatever I have done, it was the Holy Spirit in me. I know who I was. I was so weak before, so all the glory goes to Jesus. I am nothing; Jesus is everything. Without Jesus, I am the same [sinful, addicted] person that I was before."[10]

God reset not only Iman's heart and life but also his vision. Through the lens of faith-filled sight, he saw every trial and circumstance filled with holy purpose and gospel-centered intent.

LARGER THAN LIFE

As Iman learned, allowing God's perspective to transform our own illuminates even the darkest circumstances. Imagine being in the sandals of the Hebrew teenager, David, sent to take food to his three older brothers who were soldiers in the Israelite army. Suddenly, the booming voice of a larger-than-life warrior blasts through the Valley of Elah where the two sides—the Philistines and the Israelites—have lined up, ready for battle. Goliath repeats the taunt he had made before David's arrival: "I defy the ranks of Israel this day. Give me a man, that we may fight together" (1 Samuel 17:10).

Many of us know what happens next. When no one else volunteers to fight this Philistine warrior, young David does. Where others see defeat, David sees opportunity as he looks at the situation through God's eyes. Where others see their weakness, David sees God's power. And where others see the impossible, David sees a miracle.

David sees with an eternal perspective that this is the moment for God to make his kingdom evident. This lens allows him to view the battle for what it is: a turning point in history, a spiritual marker in the lives of his family and his people.

But many Bible teachers see only what an initial glance reveals: an underdog defeating a threatening warrior. They emphasize the individualistic application that, with God, we too can fell our giants. Very subtly, this application suggests a society that says, "Our nation is good and favored by God; other nations are evil and undeserving of his favor."

Although God does sometimes allow us to fell our giants, this simplistic lesson falls short of the true treasure found in God's Word. Those with eternal perspective see a deeper, more expansive truth.

> Then David said to the Philistine, "You come to me with a sword and with a spear and with a javelin, but I come to you in the name of the LORD of hosts, the God of the armies of Israel, whom you have defied. This day the LORD will deliver you into my hand, and I will strike you down and cut off your head. And I will give the dead bodies of the host of the Philistines this day to the birds of the air and to the wild beasts of the earth, that all the earth may know that there is a God in Israel" (1 Samuel 17:45–46).

When viewed through the lens of heroic faith, this oft-told children's story reveals that the collision between Israelite David and Philistine Goliath had less to do with a self-absorbed conquering of personal giants and more to do with God's redemptive purpose. David encountered and defeated this Philistine warrior "that all the earth may know that there is a God in Israel." The iconic battle reveals God's rule and reign, his kingdom at hand, to the nations of the world—from the time the conflict took place to the present day.

Elisabeth Elliot and Rachel Saint viewed their loved ones' deaths with an eternal perspective rather than personal devastation. God turned tragedy into opportunity as they, like young David, followed with eyes of heroic faith and pursued his redemptive purpose, regardless of the cost.

"I would never go because I thought it would be 'safe'—or for any other reason, such as 'carrying on my husband's work' or whatever," Elisabeth Elliot wrote in a letter to supporters of her decision to return to live and serve among the Aucas. "There is one reason alone: I believe it is simply the next step. It is the thing required at the moment."[11]

Pastor Han's eternal perspective allowed him to continue serving his friend Sang-chul and sharing the gospel with thousands despite the constant threat of an oppressive regime. We can only imagine Pastor Han's joy at the view he now has of heaven's glories, all earthly joys and sorrows rendered dim. And as God transformed Sang-Chul's outlook through his pastor friend's example, the new follower of Christ moved from a self-focused fear to an eternity-driven faith.

When the apostle Paul addressed the Athenians, who seemingly had a temple to every god or goddess imaginable, he declared, "'I perceive that in every way you are very religious'" (Acts 17:22).

At first glance, we might assume those Athenians were different from the majority of today's people, those considered to be secular ("earthly and worldly," to use biblical terms). However, whether or not they recognize it, most people today practice a sort of religion associated with their secular beliefs. Their desires firmly fixed on the fallen world, they consume information about it with near-devout devotion—all from a perspective that excludes any notion of God's power, plans, and purposes. This viewpoint lends itself to a secularist system of beliefs and practices that denies and even blasphemes the eternal—in other words, a powerful religion.

Do the pursuits and pleasures of this world dominate our lives via mass media and the devices that support it? Do we offer each day's thoughts, time, and energy to consuming our earthly affections and then discussing them with others? Do we spend our time chasing the temporal and neglecting the eternal?

If so, we have fixed our eyes on the wrong kingdom. We have laid down the pursuit of biblical discipleship and settled for something much easier—but much less real. We have abandoned an eternal perspective and become consumed by one that embraces a lesser kingdom and a lesser glory.

"DO NOT FEAR"

February 29, 1948, began on a leisurely note as Richard Wurmbrand bent down to kiss his wife, Sabina, and stepped from his home into the brisk Bucharest air. The tall, thirty-nine-year-old pastor set out on his short stroll to church, winding from Olteni Street through the picturesque Vacaresti neighborhood.

The familiar walk took him by parked cars, but Richard saw few other signs of life at that early hour. The quiet Sunday venture freed his mind to think about the main points of his morning sermon while the historic buildings flanking the street reminded him of Romania's rich history. He zigzagged his way to his church, where his wife would meet him in half an hour. Later that afternoon, he would officiate the wedding of their young friends. But for now, he followed his normal Sunday morning routine.

But that routine came to an abrupt halt when two men jumped out of a large black van and grabbed him. There would be no meeting his wife, no preaching his sermon, no officiating the afternoon wedding. Moments later, a cadre of Communist secret police forced him into the back seat of the van with a gun at his temple. As the vehicle barreled down the street toward an unknown destination, Richard stole glimpses of his surroundings through the windows.

He couldn't tear his thoughts from the politician who had committed suicide in prison only weeks after his kidnapping and arrest. *Will I suffer the same fate?* he wondered. But then he remembered a truth he had discovered earlier that year: The phrase "Do not fear" occurs exactly 366 times in the Bible, one time per day for an entire year, including leap year.

For Richard, it was providential that he was abducted on February 29, a reminder that he wouldn't need to fear what men could do to him. Fear was one emotion he would not allow to enter his prison cell. With God's help, he could endure torture, ill treatment, disease, and even death so long as others could see Christ in his eyes.

Once at their headquarters, the police manhandled Richard. They ripped off his tie, emptied his pockets of identification and papers, and stripped off his clothes. The laces of his shoes—which prisoners often used to hang themselves—were roughly removed.

This prison beneath one of Bucharest's main streets, Calea Rahovei, was new and relatively unknown. As its first prisoner, Richard knew his church members and the Romanian underground would never think to look for him here.

His concrete cell was narrow and primitive. A small box of sunlight entered the room from the window positioned too high in the wall for prisoners to escape. Richard sat on a plank bed next to a bucket in the corner and waited for the interrogators. The waiting was the hardest part of prison—the hellish part. He imagined the questions his captors would hurl at him and the torture techniques they would apply to weaken his resistance.

The threat of physical pain had extracted information from other prisoners, but the fear Richard felt during his abduction was gone. In its place was a hardened resolve to suffer anything for the sake of the gospel. Richard believed God would empower him to stand up to the worst physical agony his abductors could impart.

"I know what fear is well enough, but at that moment I felt none," Richard would later write. "This arrest, and all that would follow, was the answer to a prayer I had made, and I hoped that it would give new meaning to my past life."

Richard sat in silence. Motionless as the stones surrounding him, he thanked God for bringing him to this prison. Each passing second became an answer to his and Sabina's prayers to let them bear a cross for the sake of Christ. What strange and wonderful opportunity would blossom within these walls? What friendships with the guards could he build? Richard didn't know. But he hoped God would shine through him as he suffered in isolation.

Biblical disciples see God's kingdom at work in every circumstance, trial, and moment of their lives. With intentionality, they embrace God's sovereign passion and purpose at any cost. They see with a lens that changes their ideas, motives, and actions, recognizing that his ways are the highest and best (Isaiah 55:8–9).

May their eternal perspective be ours.

FOR REFLECTION AND DISCUSSION:

1. Do you think Elisabeth Elliot's decision to return to serve the tribe that killed her husband reflects heroic faith? If so, how? If not, why not?
2. What do you think your fellow Christians might learn from Pastor Han's example?
3. Read Hebrews 11. This chapter reminds us that God gives each of us the opportunity to have heroic faith—not just people we consider spiritual superstars. Whose name (other than those highlighted in this chapter) comes to mind when you think of heroic faith, and why?
4. How would you explain to a new Christian what it means to see with eternal perspective? What questions might he or she ask? How would you answer those questions?
5. In light of this chapter's teaching, what is God saying to you about how your own perspective might need to change?

Visit vom.org/HeroicFaith to view Sang-chul's story along with additional brief feature videos and digital resources.

HEROIC FAITH

CHAPTER 2

DEPEND ON GOD ALONE

"I see that you are powerful. And probably you have papers and documents there about me that I've never seen and can decide my fate. But God keeps records, too, and neither you nor I would have life without Him. So whether He keeps me here or sets me free, I'll accept that as best for me."

—Sabina Wurmbrand

We don't receive heroic faith in a gift-wrapped package dropped from heaven; in fact, we may not even know when God is developing it within us. That's because this powerful type of faith is not only something we possess—it's something we live.

While Richard Wurmbrand was still serving his prison sentence, his wife, Sabina, experienced the treasures such a faith produces while she was imprisoned during the Communist occupation of Romania. She wrote of a prison official's harsh interrogation in her book, *The Pastor's Wife*:

> "You're an honest woman. You can raise your price. Judas was a fool to sell his boss for thirty pieces of silver. He could have held out for 300. Tell us what you want? Freedom for you and

> your husband? A good parish for him? We'd look after your family. You could be very valuable to us. Well?"
>
> When he had finished talking there was a silence in the room. At last, I broke it.
>
> "Thanks, but I've sold myself already. The Son of God was tortured and gave His life for me. Through Him I can reach heaven. Can you offer a higher price than that?"

Sabina's boldness pointed not only to the price Christ paid on the cross but also to his power in a life surrendered to him. The heroic faith displayed by Sabina and the Christians imprisoned alongside her enabled them to face horrific challenges with grace, to respond to the darkest circumstances with peace and encouragement rather than the hatred and despair exhibited by those whose lives carried no hope of eternity.

Yet, that faith did not arise only in the squalid, overcrowded prison cells. Like a wildflower blossoming amid miles of cement, it had grown almost unnoticed as Sabina's dependence upon God increased through the years. The many hardships she had endured prior to prison drew her to Christ as her sole source of security.

After numerous weeks of confinement, something unexpected happened to the female prisoners. Officials began marching small groups of them to the camp office, then driving them away in trucks. Those left behind didn't know what was happening, but they still considered it a sign of hope. Sabina described what happened next:

> Eventually, my turn came. The major behind the desk was stout and pink as a baby. He had hands like fat little bunches

of sausages and with them he kept clearing the objects on his desk while he talked, as if he might need to jump up on it later to round off his speech.

There were a few special questions reserved for religious prisoners.

"In this place, Mrs. Wurmbrand, you must know that I am more powerful than God. At least, He has not so far made any interventions in this office." He took as his due the appreciative smiles of the two assistants. "But have you really accepted this? Have you really seen through the sham of religion? Have you realized that in a Communist society, God is superfluous? That you don't need Him anymore? If you are ever released from here, you'll be astonished at the achievements of recent years, and we are only beginning!"

The gold braid on his epaulettes was new and glistening. Under his sausage-hand was a buff file stuffed with papers which might be mine.

I said, "I see that you are powerful. And probably you have papers and documents there about me that I've never seen and can decide my fate. But God keeps records, too, and neither you nor I would have life without Him. So whether He keeps me here or sets me free, I'll accept that as best for me."

The major banged both fists on the desk, as if it were something he could hurt. "Ungrateful, Mrs. Wurmbrand, ungrateful! I'm sorry to see that you've failed to learn your lesson, and I shall make a report to that effect." He shouted in mock rage for a few minutes.

But three days later my name was read out. Higher authorities than the major were, indeed, deciding my future.

TRUE INDEPENDENCE

Sabina's bravery in the face of harsh treatment captures the core of heroic faith and points to her dependence on an authority much higher than the major or any other official. Only a heart fully surrendered to God could have endured the constant atrocities of life in a prison camp and yet shine for Christ the way Sabina's did. Only a heart that knew God as its source of security could have rested in freedom, not fear, amid imprisonment. Now as then, only hearts that recognize their dependence on God alone can enjoy true freedom against the world and its entanglements, whether marked by pleasure or pain.

When we first meet Old Testament hero Jacob, one of Isaac and Rebekah's twin sons, he demonstrates anything but dependence on God. Grasping and holding onto his twin's heel during the birth process, he reveals the character that prompted his name, which means "heel" or "supplanter" (Genesis 25:26).

Deception of one kind or another seems to be the prevailing pattern throughout Jacob's life. He conspires with his mother to cheat his twin, Esau, out of his birthright (Genesis 27:18–41. He later finds himself on the receiving end of deception when his father-in-law, Laban, famously substitutes his older daughter, Leah, for the younger one, Rachel, for whom Jacob had served Laban for seven years (Genesis 29:15–30).

God also protected Jacob in the face of Laban's deception. Even though Laban "cheated me and changed my wages ten times," the verse continues "… God did not permit him to harm me" (Genesis 31:7). Even though Jacob's bent for deception is turned back on him, the God of the covenant blessed Jacob through prospering his flocks. In the midst of consequences for his own deception, Jacob saw God's providence.

But Jacob was rescued from his duplicitous ways when, about to see Esau for the first time in many years, he spends an entire night wrestling with God. He leaves this encounter with a new name, Israel ("He strives with God"), and a limp that, for the rest of his life, serves as a reminder of the night that yielded a new relationship with God (Genesis 32:22–32).

No longer would Jacob need to lie and manipulate to gain his way; instead, he spent his remaining years following God's way. Hebrews 11:21 tells us that, as a dying old man extending a blessing to Joseph's two sons, he "bowed in worship over the head of his staff," signifying his trust in and dependence on God. Jacob moved from stealing a blessing to giving a blessing, from wrestling with God to worshiping him, and from selfish independence to a new dependence on God—one that grew his faith to heroic proportions.

PERSECUTED, NOT ABANDONED

Far removed in time and place from Jacob's journey as well as the Communist torture the Wurmbrands endured, the roughly four million Christians (just 2% of the population) who live in the Islamic Republic of Pakistan face the unthinkable because of their faith. Christian converts from Islam and those born into Christian families endure persecution in ways that range from beating, lynching, imprisonment, and even murder to the more subtle but equally destructive economic and societal oppression—all because of their faith in Jesus Christ.

In Pakistan, this harsh treatment can come from local communities, Islamic extremist groups, and the government, largely under the auspices of the country's controversial anti-blasphemy laws, which provide penalties ranging from fines to the death sentence. At any time, a Pakistani Christian can be accused of blaspheming Islam, the Quran, or Muhammad, and the law does not protect them against false accusations. Christianity is seen as a threat to Islam, Pakistan's official state religion, and as members of the minority religion, all Christians are considered expendable.

Nadia placed her trust in Christ when she was eleven years old. She quickly discovered that even family ties did not protect her from the harsh consequences faced by those who renounce Islam; in fact, family members were the source of much of her persecution. When her brother, Miled, found her praying and later going to church, he flew into a rage and began beating her weekly, insisting that she deny her newfound Savior.

She refused.

Miled followed Nadia to church one morning, caught up with her, grabbed her by the back of the neck, took her home, and beat her.

"How dare you enter that church!" he exclaimed. "Have you forgotten that you are a Muslim? You're never to set foot in that church again!"

When Nadia protested that she should be free to attend church, her brother's violence escalated. He slammed a wooden bowl into her forehead, and as she bled, he shoved her into her bedroom and locked the door. Keeping her there for weeks, he only returned to give her small amounts of food and water—but many welts and bruises. None of her family members objected to his brutality or did anything to relieve her suffering.

Eventually, she escaped and found refuge with a pastor and his family. But as a former Muslim, her presence put others at risk, and they asked her to find another place to live. When she wanted to be baptized, three pastors turned her down, again out of fear of reprisal. Eventually, a pastor in a distant Pakistani town agreed to baptize Nadia, and she discovered a newfound happiness.

God later blessed her with a Christian husband, but even then, she did not escape her family's wrath. When her parents learned of the marriage, they filed kidnapping charges against her husband. And when Miled found the couple, he beat Nadia's husband so badly his eardrum ruptured. Because the two had to remain hidden, Nadia's husband had trouble finding work until fellow Christians helped him start a business that allowed him to earn money and still avoid discovery.

Throughout the years of brutality, rejection by her family, and false accusations, Nadia remained steadfast in her faith. Her words during a time of prayer with a fellow Christian display her overwhelming dependence on God alone: "Oh Jesus, Son of God, you know me very well. You saved my husband's life when my brother attacked him and beat him badly. When we were hungry, you provided meals and a place to live. Jesus, we trust that you will never leave us. Amen."

But the challenges Pakistani Christians endure are not limited to violent persecution. Unless they renounce Christ, their only employment opportunities consist of undesirable, labor-intensive jobs. Many are trapped in financial schemes that, from birth, place them in permanent bondage to their Muslim employers. Women in particular suffer from this type of bondage, and some face the additional threat of forced marriage to a Muslim. Whether male or female, all live in the land of no opportunity:

- John sweeps up trash in his village's dusty streets, ostracized by those he encounters, trapped in a societal prison for the crime of faith in Christ.
- Samuel, a day laborer, stamps out brick after molded brick in the burning Pakistani sun, knowing his Christian faith leaves him with no hope of a better job.
- Paul, whose job requires him to lower himself into a succession of sewage pits to bring forth buckets of foul-smelling sludge, scrubs himself in an outdoor shower to remove the filth—realizing that his faith means he, too, has no hope of vocational advancement.
- Sarah cares for another family's home and children, performing the most menial tasks while denied any of the comforts enjoyed by the family she serves. Yet her continual dependence on God yields a joy that shines through her circumstances.

One front-line Christian worker described the attitude of Christians in Pakistan this way:

> But we have a church, where Christians come together to worship the Lord Jesus Christ. To sing his praise, to study his Word. For while our country has turned its back on us, God has not. Sometimes it is not easy—the loss, the injustice, so please remember to pray for us, that we will continue to live together in fellowship. That we will continue to see the joy of the Lord in our lives. And that we will persevere in our faith, no matter the cost. And please remember we are praying for you.

Despite the cost, all these believers boldly proclaim their faith. They come together in worship, thanks, and praise. And they pray for their brothers and sisters in Christ across the globe, trusting that those family members are also interceding on their behalf.

Many living in other countries would protest such injustices, but our Pakistani brothers and sisters have no voice in government. This is part of the oppression they endure every day. However, it is also an opportunity to trust God alone. Rather than declare independence from the government—which would place them in a no-win situation—like Jacob, these humble men and women demonstrate their moment-by-moment dependence on the great Creator God.

PRAYER-BORN DEPENDENCE

The term *humble* also applies to Brother Lawrence, a seventeenth-century monk who, as a lay brother in the Carmelite order, spent much of his religious service in the kitchen. It was there he learned one of the secrets to true dependence on God: remaining in a constant attitude of prayer. He termed this "practicing the presence of God." A fellow monk, who sought to learn the source of his brother's spiritual strength, compiled a book of letters from and conversations with him on this topic. It remains in print today.[1]

For Brother Lawrence, prayer went far beyond the prescribed practices of his faith. It included talking to God while mopping the kitchen floor, peeling potatoes, or carrying out other menial tasks. Weeding the garden moved him to speak to God about his desire to weed out the character weeds so prominent in his life. Scrubbing pots led him to reflect on God's cleansing power:

> It is a great delusion to think our times of prayer ought to differ from other times: that we are as strictly obliged to adhere to God by action in the time of action as by prayer in its season. ...[2]
>
> There is not in the world a kind of life more sweet and delightful than that of a continual conversation with God: those only can comprehend it who practice and experience it. ...[3]

Many believers practice a crisis-based relationship with God, resorting to prayer only in the case of "emergencies." But Brother Lawrence recognized the radical truth: daily, moment-by-moment dependence on God, especially in the most mundane moments, yields a habit of increasing reliance upon him that will bear fruit in the deepest darkness and most prevailing pressure. He saw what he called the "common business" of everyday life as the transmitter for pure and passionate dependence on God, writing, "The time of business does not differ with me from the time of prayer; and in the noise and clatter of my kitchen, while several persons are at the same time calling for different things, I possess God in as great tranquility as if I were on my knees. ..."[4]

When we follow Brother Lawrence's example of having a continual conversation with God (rather than calling on him only in times of crisis), listening for his voice, and looking for his work, we will find that God uses our fresh awareness to prepare us for the difficult times in our life.

Not all who have demonstrated heroic faith have been privileged to read Brother Lawrence's book, but they have all discovered his secret. By maintaining a conscious dependence on the Lord, they prove the truth of the apostle Paul's injunction to "pray without ceasing," which in turn equips them to "give thanks in all circumstances" (1 Thessalonians 5:17–18).

FROM DOUBT TO DEPENDENCE

We all face choices every day, but few come with the extreme repercussions that Dinaw, who lives in Ethiopia, had to consider when placing his faith in Christ. Imprisoned for assaulting a neighbor, he was serving a three-year sentence when two fellow prisoners shared the gospel with him. Fearing violent persecution if he abandoned his Muslim faith, Dinaw was reluctant to believe. But as he came to understand the good news, he made a decision to follow Jesus.

Soon, family members who worked as police officers reported his "heretical" beliefs to his father, who gathered Dinaw's brothers and friends to visit the prison and confront him. Dinaw told them he had given his life to Jesus.

Dinaw's family was incensed that he had become a Christian, in their view a *penti*, a derogatory term for a biblical Christian whom they consider to be an infidel.

Furious, his father returned home and wrote a letter to the police chief, urging him to keep his son in prison even after his sentence ended. But Dinaw had a surprising response: "I like prison," he told the guards. "I can read my Bible every day here, so don't worry about that."

After his eventual release, the threats of violence began, taking eighteen months to come to fruition. One night, while Dinaw was sleeping in a field to care for one of his cows, a group of villagers came to his home. They tied the door shut, trapping his sleeping wife and children inside.

The smell of smoke awakened Dinaw, and he saw his home burning only a few hundred yards away. He rushed to the house, untied the rope, and rescued his family from the flames. But once again, Dinaw had a surprising response. This man, who had once rejected Christ out of fear of retribution, now spoke words that demonstrated his full dependence on God:

> I was not upset when my home was destroyed, because I knew the Lord had led me to sleep with my cows to be able to save my family. … My life belongs to God, and I believe He put me here. I don't know why He wants me to stay here, but I believe He is working. If He allows me to be killed, I am ready to die. If He wants to save the entire village, then I have to just be patient.

PERSECUTION AND POWER

Like Dinaw's case, persecution was a way of life for the early Christians, and so was continual dependence on their heavenly Father. The same Holy Spirit who called Paul and Barnabas on what became known as Paul's first missionary journey, also empowered them for the intense opposition they would face along the way (see Acts 13:1–3).

When that missionary calling took place, the five men mentioned, including Paul and Barnabas, were "fasting and praying" (v. 3). The verb tense indicates that this was not a one-time event but the regular practice of these disciples. Our habits expose what we value most, which in this case was complete dependence on Jesus Christ, in whom Paul would later say "we live and move and have our being" (Acts 17:28).

This dependence reveals itself all the way through Paul and Barnabas' travels as evidenced by the divine presence, power, and wisdom that guided and accompanied the two wherever they went. By the time they reached the pagan city of Iconium, both satanic and religious forces appeared solidly aligned against them (Acts 14). In fact, in the previous chapter, they met with such opposition from the Jewish leaders that they were forcibly driven out of the area, famously shaking the "dust from their feet" against their misguided opponents while "filled with joy and with the Holy Spirit" (Acts 13:51–52).

The Holy Spirit, and the constant dependence on him, led them next to do the unthinkable. Their first stop in Iconium was the synagogue, where they willingly placed themselves back in the midst of potential Jewish hostility.

Indeed, God used the two in a mighty way, and the pattern of people coming to faith amid rising persecution continued:

> Now at Iconium they entered together into the Jewish synagogue and spoke in such a way that a great number of both Jews and Greeks believed. But the unbelieving Jews stirred up the Gentiles and poisoned their minds against the brothers. So they remained for a long time, speaking boldly for the Lord, who bore witness to the word of his grace, granting signs and wonders to be done by their hands. But the people of the city were divided; some sided with the Jews and some with the apostles (Acts 14:1–4).

Paul and Barnabas then relived their previous traumatic experience as, learning of a plot to flog and stone them, they fled Iconium for a new place of ministry in the cities of Lystra and Derbe. Still, their unwavering dependence on God—a key catalyst to heroic faith—meant their next choice was equally predictable: "and there they continued to preach the gospel" (Acts 14:7).

LEARNING TO DOUBT OUR DOUBTS

As we saw in the previous chapter, those who model heroic faith draw upon an invisible reality; they see life from God's point of view. But even the most focused among us will still have doubts, especially during lonely nights of hardship and suffering. Separated from family and friends, surrounded by enemies, we can wonder, *Where is God?* or *What is God doing?* or even *Why me?* That's what makes those of heroic faith so remarkable—even during their darkest days, they depend completely on their Lord.

"They can say whatever they want. If I am to die, then I am willing to die." That's what Sun, a Christian from the Khmu ethnic group in Laos, told herself when her bold proclamation moved village officials to summon her as well as her friend and fellow believer, Vee, to the village office for questioning.

Vee, older but with Spirit-birthed spunk, rebuffed the authorities. "Why do you keep bothering me about this? Do you not have eyes? I was very ill. I prayed, Christians came to pray for me, and I was healed. Of course, I will go worship the One who healed me and fellowship with the Christians."

These two courageous women, subsequently removed from their village and forced to find alternative housing because of their faith, had the strength to doubt their doubts and depend entirely on God. Through their newfound dependence on God's Word, they continued embracing the life-changing truth of the gospel despite the hardships they endured.

We may not find ourselves imprisoned like the Wurmbrands, beaten and rejected like Nadia, trapped in menial labor like modern Pakistani believers, having our home set on fire like Dinaw, or cast out of our community like Vee and Sun, but other forms of darkness can dim our sense of God's presence. We wonder, *Does he love me? Does he care?*

When darkness surrounds us, we must seek the light. And as Brother Lawrence discovered, when we "practice his presence" via the disciplines of prayer and spending time with God, we live in constant dependence upon him. That is when our faith grows to heroic proportions. We follow the same pattern of surrender demonstrated by Paul and Barnabas: be filled with the Spirit and empty of doubt, rejoicing in God no matter the cost.

FOR REFLECTION AND DISCUSSION:

1. How did Sabina Wurmbrand display her dependence on God?
2. What do you think Brother Lawrence meant by the following: "It is a great delusion to think our times of prayer ought to differ from other times"?
3. Which biblical figure comes to mind when you first think of the phrase *dependence on God*? Why?
4. Which Pakistani believer's story inspires you the most? Explain how and why it spoke to you.
5. What purpose did Jacob's limp—acquired from his time of wrestling with God—serve? What "limp" have you developed as you have wrestled with God and, in the process, become more dependent upon him?

6. Can you declare with Dinaw, "my life belongs to God"? How does that type of understanding give you a more eternal perspective as you view the circumstances you experience?

Visit vom.org/HeroicFaith to view stories of Pakistani believers along with additional brief feature videos and digital resources.

HEROIC FAITH

CHAPTER 3

TRUST GOD'S WORD

"I recite Bible verses to myself, but the words are getting harder and harder to remember. I can handle the torture, the starvation, but I desperately need my Bible. Every day I pray over and over for God to give me a Bible."

—Boun, an imprisoned Laotian Christian

Throughout recorded history, the truth of God's Word has challenged heresies and false religions too many times to count. Yet the greatest conflict may rest in the hearts of individual believers who must decide what they will do with the Scriptures. Will they believe them? Will they receive their truth? Will they act on their teachings or set them aside as but one more opinion to accept or reject on a whim?

Those with heroic faith share the common characteristics of seeing with eternal perspective and depending on God alone. Now, we must add another foundational characteristic that both identifies them and serves to build within them a deeper heroic faith: unconditional trust in the Word of God and its life-giving truths.

Timothy and Maura, first-century believers, newlyweds, and residents of the Roman province of Mauritania in West Africa, lived out that trust. When Governor Arrianus sent soldiers to search out copies of the sections of the Bible (Scriptures) owned by their church, Timothy refused to comply—and paid for it via tremendous suffering.

First, soldiers burned out his eyes with hot irons. Then he was hung upside down with a heavy weight around his neck.

Maura was in agony as she watched Timothy suffer, pleading with him to reveal the location of the Scriptures.

As Timothy waited for his tormentors to remove his gag, God replaced his fear with holy calm and Spirit-empowered boldness. Instead of renouncing his faith and disclosing the location of God's Word, Timothy urged his young wife, "Do not let your love for me come before your love for Christ."

His courage strengthened Maura's own resolve, and she declared that she was prepared to die with Timothy.

Enraged by Timothy's refusal and Maura's newfound courage, the governor sentenced the pair to the harshest tortures of the Roman world—yet they refused to deny their Savior. At one point, when onlookers demanded a halt to Maura's abuse, this innocent woman boldly proclaimed her dependence upon God alone. Eventually, the faithful pair was crucified, side by side, united not only by death but also by their enduring trust in their Lord and in his Word.

DEADLY DEVOTION

Of course, Timothy and Maura are not alone as those who lived out their trust in the deep truths of God's Word. Centuries later, in 1519 near Coventry, England, six men and a widow were convicted of an extreme crime against the church. That offense? Teaching their children the Lord's Prayer, the Ten Commandments, and the Apostle's Creed in the English language.

At that time, Latin was the only language allowed for biblical instruction in England; yet the common people spoke English. Refusing to obey authorities, Christians secretly translated parts of the Bible into English, carefully passing the translations from home to home. These seven were caught, convicted, and sentenced to be burned at the stake.

At the end of the proceedings, the widow was pardoned and allowed to go free. She had young children to raise, so no one protested the decision. But as a guard walked her home, he heard a rustling in the woman's coat sleeve. He discovered the English translations, the same materials the convicted believers had been teaching their children. Even though this woman had just escaped a death sentence, she refused to part with the precious documents, believing that her children still needed to know the truth of God's Word in their language.

This profound act sealed her fate. Soon after, she and the six men were secured to wooden poles and burned alive.

William Tyndale lived in an era when the church in England had banned the hand-copied work of John Wycliffe—the only English-language Bible in the world—making it a crime to own this text. One day in the early 1520s, Tyndale, an Oxford- and Cambridge-educated scholar and former priest, engaged in a heated discussion with a learned theologian.

"Master Tyndale, you must admit that men are better with the laws of the church that they can understand than God's own law in the Bible!" the doctor of theology scoffed.

"I defy the priests and their law!" Tyndale responded. "If God sees fit to let me live, then it won't be long before any boy who drives a plough will know the Scriptures better than they do!"

This remark divided Tyndale and the established church. He made the challenging choice to make God's Word more accessible to the common man. He trusted God's Word—and he demonstrated that trust with his life.

Tyndale decided to translate from the Greek and Hebrew texts to create a Bible in the common language of the people. He wanted a translation so readable and accurate that an Englishman could depend on it, learn from it, and find God's voice in it.

To accomplish this, Tyndale had to leave England, where, with no support from the established clergy, his life would be in danger. He completed his English translation of the New Testament in Germany in 1525. For years, these small New Testaments were smuggled in bales of cotton, aboard German ships, and by any other means they could be smuggled into England.

Tyndale next traveled to Antwerp, Belgium, where he translated and printed the first five books of the Old Testament. He was just a few steps ahead of the English agents seeking both him and the bounty offered for his capture. Tyndale was befriended on false pretenses and then betrayed to authorities who arrested and imprisoned him in 1535 at the castle at Vilvoorde, near Brussels. There he suffered in dank, cold conditions for eighteen months before standing trial for "maintaining that faith alone justifies . . . that to believe in the forgiveness of sins, and to embrace the mercy offered in the gospel, was enough for salvation."

Aware that these charges could lead only to his death, Tyndale worked during his imprisonment to complete his Bible translations. Condemned as a heretic in August 1536, he was defrocked and kept at Vilvoorde for two more months before being tied to a stake with brush piled around him. Before an executioner snapped the rope that would strangle him prior to the flames consuming his body, Tyndale was heard to pray, "Lord, open the king of England's eyes."

Two years later, God answered that prayer. King Henry VIII authorized the distribution of the Matthew Bible, much of which was Tyndale's work. In 1539, the same king ordered all printers and booksellers to provide for the "free and liberal use of the Bible in our own maternal English tongue." Because of William Tyndale and his dogged determination to deliver the Bible to the masses, many more people had the opportunity to know and trust God's Word.

STANDING ON THE PROMISES

The life story of Old Testament faith hero Joseph captures every reader's attention. From the early battles with his brothers to rising in the ranks as a slave to false accusations, imprisonment, and more, the account of his life introduces readers to God's faithfulness.

We might be surprised that the writer of Hebrews, under the Spirit's guidance, chose Joseph's deathbed request in Genesis 50:24–25—a seemingly obscure segment of his life—to highlight as an example of heroic faith: "By faith Joseph, at the end of his life, made mention of the exodus of the Israelites and gave directions concerning his bones" (Hebrews 11:22).

Even renowned seventeenth-century preacher Charles Spurgeon was surprised. In a sermon titled, "Joseph's Bones," Spurgeon explained:

> The Holy Spirit in this chapter selects out of good men's lives the most brilliant instances of their faith. I should hardly have expected that he would have mentioned the dying scene of Joseph's life as the most illustrious proof of his faith in God.

> That eventful life—perhaps the most interesting in all sacred Scripture, with the exception of one, abounds with incidents, of which the Holy Spirit might have said by his servant Paul, "By faith Joseph did this and that," but none is mentioned save the closing scene. The triumph especially of his chastity under well-known and exceedingly severe temptation, might have been very properly traced to the power of his faith, but it is passed over, and the fact that he gave commandment concerning his bones is singled out as being the most illustrious proof of his faith. Does not this tell us, dear brethren and sisters, that we are very poor judges of what God will most delight in? Very likely when we least please ourselves God is best pleased with us.[1]

Spurgeon and others look into the text with divine insight to extract the reason Joseph's dying words serve as an example of heroic faith—and of the trust in God's Word that helped build it. The patriarch did not make his dying request out of a misguided yearning for memorialization or even a longing to be buried with his family as his father, Jacob, displayed (Genesis 49:29–30). Instead, Joseph's words rose from a heart that trusted fully in God's Word, because he fully trusted the God who brought the Israelites out of Egypt.

This word was first spoken to Moses and Aaron as a promise recorded in both Genesis 15, where God first lays out his covenant, as well as in the book of Exodus: "I have come down to deliver them out of the hand of the Egyptians and to bring them up out of that land to a good and broad land, a land flowing with milk and honey, to the place of the Canaanites, the Hittites, the Amorites, the Perizzites, the Hivites, and the Jebusites" (Exodus 3:8).

Joseph did not have a Bible or even a hand-copied scroll to study to determine God's will and ways. What he did have was an abiding trust in the God who made the promises—a trust that his Word was and would be true, even four hundred years down the desert road, when Israel at last took possession of the Promised Land (Joshua 11:23, 21:43–45).

DESPERATE NEED

Following the pattern set by Joseph, those with true heroic faith live out their abiding trust in the Word of God. Like Boun of Laos, they demonstrate that trust by clinging to Scripture regardless of personal cost.

"I am in prison for telling others about Jesus."

Boun's understated declaration could not begin to capture the violent treatment he suffered at the hands of the Communist regime. Handcuffed, feet bound to a board, he was left in solitary confinement by his captors who dragged him out only for harsh interrogation sessions. One day, after accusing him of being an American spy, a prison official screamed at him, "Write your confession now! Write it! Confess, or I will have you shot!"

The gun held to Boun's head during this confrontation did not have the power to pull him from his devotion to the Lord; however, it did highlight his critical need for the Word of God. "I don't know why they didn't shoot me," he said. "I am losing hope and fear I have been forgotten. . . . I recite Bible verses to myself, but the words are getting harder and harder to remember. I can handle the torture, the starvation, but I desperately need my Bible. Every day I pray over and over for God to give me a Bible."

Years later, after the guards had come to trust him, Boun devised a complicated plan to return home to retrieve (and hide) copies of the

Scriptures while out collecting firewood as part of his prison duties. “It is very risky, but God is answering my prayer,” he said. “I will risk everything to have a Bible.”

When he returned to the prison with firewood, he also brought one of the contraband Bibles, miraculously overlooked by the guard who inspected his bag. Boun knew God had intervened.

But his delight in devouring Scripture lasted only a short season. A guard discovered his hidden Bible and, enraged, ripped it apart.

“They found my Bible, but I will not give up,” Boun said. “I will bring in more Bibles. I will read God’s Word every chance I get.”

He remained in prison for ten more years before he was finally released. “When I read my Bible, I am encouraged to keep fighting,” he said later. “I thank my brothers and sisters around the world who were praying for me.”

God’s Word has the power to change lives, the power to provide strength, and the power to encourage believers in their greatest joys and deepest despair. When we place our trust in his Word, we are placing our trust in everything God offers us in Christ—building toward a more heroic faith.

THE HANDWRITTEN BIBLE

What would we do without access to the Word of God? Some of us might hardly notice the loss. Others, like Houmayoun, would do anything to obtain a copy.

As Pastor Houmayoun led a prayer meeting at his home in Iran, secret police stormed in and arrested the pastor, his wife, their teenage son, and four other church leaders. The seven Christians were blindfolded, shoved into vehicles, and taken to an intelligence prison for questioning. After days of interrogation, they were moved to a public prison and ordered to keep quiet about the reason for their arrest; the guards rightly feared the spread of Christianity among the prison's six thousand inmates.

Instead of despairing over their situation, the Christians saw an opportunity to spread the gospel. As they shared their testimony quietly with one prisoner after another, they received a variety of responses. A few threatened to kill them, while others listened passively. Some, however, showed a sincere interest; one man approached the group, asked if they were Christians, and asked for more information.

"I was simply telling my testimony and telling about the good news of the gospel and stories from the Bible," Pastor Houmayoun recalled. "God gave me wisdom about who was open and how much to share."

The Christians' evangelistic efforts angered the guards, however, and Houmayoun alone received twenty written warnings to stop sharing the gospel with Muslim prisoners. But despite the threats from the guards and the inmates, the believers committed themselves to expanding God's kingdom inside the Iranian prison. Eventually, the Muslim inmates began to wonder what made these seven people so different.

Realizing they needed God's Word to help sustain them in prison, the Christians began writing memorized Bible verses on scraps of paper. They encouraged one another by sharing the verses they remembered.

"God was reminding us of these verses and strengthening us through the parts we memorized," Pastor Houmayoun said.

After several months, and with the assistance of handwritten Scripture verses smuggled into prison, the believers had complete handwritten copies of some books of the Bible to read and share. Bibles in Iran are highly restricted, but God's Word was multiplying inside the walls of that prison. After being released, Houmayoun and his family fled Iran, yet are continuing to share the gospel with Iranians via creative means.

Houmayoun's firm foundation and implicit trust in the Word of God—even without a physical copy—enabled him to endure the suffering that came because of his faith, empowering him to continue advancing God's kingdom, even while incarcerated.

STRENGTHENING THE CHURCH

We've seen how God can work even when his followers lack copies of the Bible. In many countries, access to the Scriptures is restrained or denied, sometimes by governmental pressure and sometimes by limited resources.

Ethiopia is a prime example of the latter. Considered a majority-Christian country, it is a place where many Orthodox Christians rely on their leaders as their resource for Scripture. In addition, Christians in Bible-based churches remain in great need of Bibles.

When front-line workers visited a large church in central Ethiopia and asked the congregation how many needed a Bible, most raised their hands. God's Word is essential in this country where biblical Christians are a distinct minority, harassed by militants among the Ethiopian Orthodox Church on one side and violently persecuted by radical Muslims on the other.

Front-line workers say fewer than 10% of biblical Christians possess their own Bibles. One new believer living in an area especially resistant to the gospel said he and the other nineteen members of his church had to share a single copy.

"Because we live in a rural area far from each other, we cannot come to church daily to take turns to read the Bible," he said. "So the church planter passed the one Bible around so that each member of the church could take a turn to take the Bible home to read. We returned the Bible on Fridays so that the church planter could prepare his teaching for Sunday."

When this believer and other families in his church received their own copies of the Scriptures in their native Oromo language, they rejoiced. No longer did they have to rotate a single copy. The church planter reported increased growth in the church and in the lives of individual believers as their access to and trust in the Word of God increased.

WORDS ABOUT THE WORD

The author of Psalm 119, considered by many to be King David, exhibited the same trust in God's Word that Joseph, Houmayoun, Boun, the Ethiopian biblical Christians, and countless others of heroic faith demonstrated. In fact, the entire psalm gives praise to God and his Word.

Verses 81–88 offer specific insights for those who are suffering, whether from persecution or other trials. The psalmist describes himself as "having become like a wineskin in the smoke" (v. 83), which seems to point to the impact of life's harsher circumstances. Our spirits become dried up by what we have endured, much like a soft, pliable wineskin becomes dried and brittle by hanging in smoke. But even as he faces extreme suffering, the psalmist is careful to note, "yet I have not forgotten your statutes" (v. 83). His trust in the Word of God continues to sustain him despite his trials, which also continue as the psalm progresses.

"How long must your servant endure?" he wonders (v. 84). Regardless of the answer, he holds to his trust in God's Word. Despite the fact his enemies attempt to harm him as well as fail to abide by God's Law, persecuting him with lies and bringing him to the edge of death, he proclaims his trust in God's precepts (vv. 85–87). The author concludes this section of the psalm with a plea for strength but with a purpose. He asks God to "give me life," not for his own self-service but that he may continue his faithfulness to and trust in his Word (v. 88).

Persecuted Christians live out the word picture painted by the author of this psalm—"like a wineskin in the smoke." Battered by opposition and harassment in an attempt to silence their witness, their bodies pay the price for heroic faith. No doubt their mouths echo the words, "How long must your servant endure?" But, like the psalmist, they continue to trust God and rely on his sustaining power despite the pain. Their testimony inspires every biblical disciple to trust God's Word no matter how he or she feels in moments of trial.

FROM MUSLIM TO MISSIONARY

It is not surprising that Ibrahim, born a Somali Muslim in Kenya, would spend time in prison for smuggling Bibles in an effort to spread the gospel. After all, his own walk of faith began when he heard God's Word.

As a policeman in the city of Mombasa, Ibrahim was assigned to observe a large crowd gathered for an evangelistic outreach. His commanding officer was concerned the event could become chaotic or the target of a potential attack, and he needed officers to keep an eye on things.

And so Ibrahim was there that day in the mid-1960s when the missionary stepped forward, took the microphone, and opened his Bible to Exodus 14. More than five decades later, Ibrahim can still hear the passion in the missionary's voice, but it was what the missionary *read* that day that held his attention: the story of the Israelites fleeing Egypt.

Ibrahim mistakenly thought the missionary was reading from the Quran, which includes its own version of the Exodus story. But why was a Christian reading and preaching from the Muslim holy book? *Is this speaker a Christian or a Muslim*? he wondered.

His curiosity drove him first to attend a church not far from the police encampment where he slept each night and then to meet with the church's pastor. "Why was your missionary speaking out of the Quran?" he asked bluntly.

After some confusion, the pastor realized Ibrahim was referring to the Book of Exodus—and gave him a copy of the Bible to aid in his understanding. Thus began Ibrahim's transformation from Muslim to follower of *Isa al Masih* (Jesus the Messiah) and from policeman to pastor. He left the police force and took another job, where a coworker—who happened to be an assistant pastor—noticed his questions and began studying the Bible with him every day. Eventually, Ibrahim went to church with his mentor and placed his faith in Christ.

Ibrahim's family was not happy about his new faith—they saw his decision as heretical and one that shamed them in the eyes of their community. His family disowned him, cutting him off from the most important group of people for any Muslim. Although Ibrahim was disowned by his earthly family, he found a new family among fellow believers. However, his wife cried for over a year about his decision to follow Christ, and her Muslim friends encouraged her to leave him.

Ibrahim faced increasing threats from his clan's local leaders, but those pressures only strengthened his desire to serve God.

After God opened the door for him to attend Bible school, Ibrahim began to smuggle Bibles across the border into Somalia. He carefully packed New Testaments into white milk cans, strapped the cans and other goods onto the back of a camel, and headed out for a seven-day ride from his home in Kenya into Somalia. He made the trip four times a year, carrying fifty New Testaments on each journey.

Ibrahim knew being caught with a Bible could mean a death sentence. Because of both the danger and the deep need, each New Testament was disassembled and distributed one page at a time after he arrived in Somalia. Despite these precautions, he endured attacks from rock-throwing Muslims during some of his smuggling trips; he was once arrested and detained for four days. But Ibrahim continued to trust that God's Word would not return void—and persisted taking it across the border. He later saw a man who had led a stoning attack against him come to faith in Christ and apologize for his actions.

However, the worst was yet to come. Ibrahim's clan forcibly removed his wife and children from him, housing them for a time at the Saudi Arabian Embassy, courtesy of the Saudi ambassador, who saw the spread and protection of Islam as a significant part of his duties. Later, relatives buried his wife of more than sixty years without even telling him she had died.

Throughout this period of darkness and discouragement, Ibrahim leaned on the church and on the power of God's Word. One passage he returned to again and again was Psalm 5, which speaks of God's care for his children as well as his punishment of those who abuse them:

> Give ear to my words, O LORD; consider my groaning. Give attention to the sound of my cry, my King and my God, for to you do I pray. . . . The boastful shall not stand before your eyes; you hate all evildoers. You destroy those who speak lies; the LORD abhors the bloodthirsty and deceitful man. . . . But let all who take refuge in you rejoice; let them ever sing for joy, and spread your protection over them, that those who love your name may exult in you. For you bless the righteous, O LORD; you cover him with favor as a shield.

"Even Paul . . . they stoned him," said Ibrahim, who has always drawn encouragement from biblical heroes of the faith. "Those who believed ahead of me, most of them suffered the same and even worse persecution. Stephen was killed because of his testimony. I realized I would have to go through the same path they suffered. Even Peter was imprisoned, and the doors [of his cell] were opened."

Northern Kenya remains dotted with living memorials to Ibrahim's trust in God's Word and determination to spread it to others; over the years of his ministry, he planted twenty-three churches. Despite hardships—including the loss of his family and being shot, stoned, and arrested twice as well as having his evangelistic meetings shut down or canceled—he does not view his sufferings as anything out of the ordinary. "If you volunteer to be a good steward of the Word of God, you will go through several problems, challenges, even through fire," he said.

More than fifty years since the Word of God kindled the initial flame in his heart, Ibrahim stood firm on his trust in God and his Word. "I'm still carrying my Bible," he said with a smile. "I must continue preaching."

PRECIOUS PATTERN

The background of longtime missionary John Short, a native Australian, is much different from Ibrahim's, yet he stands on a similar trust in the Word of God. His more than fifty-year calling and commitment to distribute Scripture in China resulted in Bibles being placed into the hands of tens of thousands of Chinese Christians.

Over time, God opened doors for his ministry in other parts of Asia: Burma, Vietnam, and even North Korea, where in 2013, officials detained him. Released thirteen days later, John signed a forced confession that included his admission that "I wanted as many North Koreans to become Christians as possible."

When he arrived in North Korea, officials first inspected the contents of his suitcase, which, as always, held a Bible right on top.

"I make a point of putting my Bible on the top, my personal Bible, on the top of my possessions," John explained. "Before each entrance [to North Korea] our possessions are investigated. If a North Korean says, 'What's that?' I say, "That's a Bible, my Bible.'

"They say, 'You can't take that into North Korea.' I say, 'If I can't take that in, I don't go in; then you will have to cancel my visit because I am a Christian. I read my Bible every day. I need this with me.'

"Then they will call in others and have a little debate about it and say, 'We shouldn't let you carry it.' I say, 'I need it. I have to have it.' I feel it is a testimony to them in this. Then they will say, 'It will be recorded. You must bring this out again.' I say, 'It's an English Bible. I don't think Koreans would enjoy it as much as I do. It is my Bible. I give you my word I will bring it out again.'"

On this trip, John's Bible would prove more important than ever. Detained by officials for leaving gospel tracts at the site of a Buddhist temple, he was allowed no contact with the outside world. But a habit he and his wife, Karen, had established years before served him well. Throughout their married life, they read the Bible each day. In addition to other passages, they read a chapter from Proverbs and a chapter from John's Gospel. On the first day of the month, they read the first chapter of those books, continuing this pattern for the rest of each month.

John couldn't call his wife and reassure her of his well-being. He couldn't hear her comforting words or encouragement. However, he said, reading those chapters every day and knowing she was reading the same words gave him a sense of spiritual connection greater than any phone line could offer.

For Karen, the familiar pattern was equally comforting. Her one prayer for John, in fact, was that he be able to keep his Bible. "I knew the Lord was in control. I didn't have a fear for him, only desiring that he would be able to have his Bible and then he would be fine. He would be able to read, he would be able to get food for his own soul in whatever situation," Karen said.

Reading God's Word. Memorizing God's Word. Trusting in God's Word. Rather than Pharisaical commands, these have become key life truths for people such as Houmayoun and Ibrahim as well as for John and Karen. All of them placed their trust in God's Word, and all saw it bring forth the fruit of heroic faith in their lives along with a dynamic impact on those around them.

FOR REFLECTION AND DISCUSSION:

1. Does the culture around you affirm or deny the truth contained in God's Word? Give examples if possible.

2. Think about a time when you have felt like "a wineskin in the smoke." What helped renew you so you could continue being faithful to God? Take time to review Psalm 119. Select some key verses about the value of God's Word to memorize, and share why you chose them.
3. Boun took great risks to smuggle the Bible into his prison cell. What does that say about how he valued God's Word? What about God's Word do you value most?
4. John Short considered the Bible an essential whenever he packed for a trip. As you travel, does the Bible have an important place in your packing? Explain why or why not. How does reading God's Word regularly build your trust in God?
5. Despite his trust in God and his Word, Ibrahim went through some dark times of discouragement. Share how God's Word has brought you comfort amid your challenging times.

Visit vom.org/HeroicFaith to view Boun's story along with additional brief feature videos and digital resources.

HEROIC FAITH

CHAPTER 4

LIVE A SACRIFICIAL LIFE

"Once I said yes to Jesus, I was committed. I was all in."
—John Allen Chau

"Thy will be done."

These simple words must have shocked the Roman soldiers who burst into Polycarp's home, intent on arresting the elderly man, whom they knew to be a devout follower of Christ. They had already slain others who claimed the name of Jesus, and at a recent execution, the crowd in the arena chanted for Polycarp's death.

Others might have fled, fought, or, at the very least, trembled in fear at the soldiers' sudden appearance. But Polycarp, who had placed his trust in his Savior under the tutelage of John the apostle, knew the Roman proconsul (governor) had been searching for him. After asking that food be brought for the soldiers, Polycarp made only one plea for himself: that he be granted an hour for prayer.

Amazed at his boldness, the soldiers granted the request. For two hours, Polycarp prayed before the soldiers escorted him to the arena to be put to death.

"Be strong, Polycarp, and act like a man," came a voice from heaven heard by Polycarp and the other Christians present. Because of Polycarp's age, the Roman proconsul gave him one final chance to live. All he had to do was swear by Caesar and say, "Take away the atheists" (At that time, Christians were called atheists for refusing to worship the Greek and Roman gods).

"Take away the atheists," Polycarp proclaimed, gesturing toward the roaring crowds.

"Swear, and I will let you go," the proconsul continued. "Reproach Christ!"

But Polycarp had no such intention. Turning back to the proconsul, he boldly declared, "Eighty-six years I have served him, and he has done me no wrong. How can I blaspheme my King who saved me?"

"Swear by the Fortune of Caesar," the proconsul urged.

Polycarp stood firm. "Since you vainly think that I will swear by the Fortune of Caesar, as you say, and pretend not to know who I am, listen carefully. I am a Christian!"

"I have wild beasts," the proconsul threatened. "I will throw you to them, if you do not repent."

"Call them!" came Polycarp's retort. "For we cannot 'repent' from what is better to what is worse, but it is noble to turn from what is evil to what is righteous."

Next, the proconsul threatened him with fire, but this only evoked a stronger response. The Romans ultimately moved him to the marketplace, preparing to burn him at the stake. Even as they readied the wood for the fire, their intended victim prayed, confessing his faith in Christ. After the prayer, the soldiers lit the pyre—but the fire formed an arch around his body. Polycarp succumbed only after they resorted to stabbing him when the fire wouldn't touch him. He died as he lived, sacrificing all for Christ.

As we have read, people of heroic faith share several common characteristics. Rather than acquiring these by chance or coincidence, they make a series of choices that ensure their lives carry each trait. God builds heroic faith within them—one deliberate choice at a time.

SUTA'S SACRIFICE

Nowhere does the process of heroic faith shine brighter than through the moment-by-moment choices Christians have made over the centuries to lay down their lives for the cause of Christ. Sometimes, as in Polycarp's case, these choices may include physical death. But they always include the self-denial Jesus commanded in Luke 9:23: "If anyone would come after me, let him deny himself and take up his cross daily and follow me." The Savior further illustrated this self-sacrifice in John 12:24: "Truly, truly, I say to you, unless a grain of wheat falls into the earth and dies, it remains alone; but if it dies, it bears much fruit."

Suta of India made choices built on self-denial, sacrificing himself and his desires for the cause of Christ—choices that nearly cost him his life. The young evangelist entered a remote village, armed with the gospel and intent on sharing the good news. When word spread of his presence, the village leadership confronted him and sent him away. "Don't come back," they told him.

But four days later, Suta returned, persisting in his attempts to share the gospel and hand out tracts to those he met. This time, the village leaders were outraged.

"What's going on?" they shouted. "Why did you come back? We are a Hindu village! We only practice Hinduism!"

"If I didn't come back, who would tell you about Jesus?"

"We don't want your Jesus! We will not listen to your message!" the men yelled, slapping and pushing Suta until they shoved him, bleeding, into a pit. There, they left him to die.

But the violence didn't keep the Holy Spirit from working. One of Suta's persecutors returned home, deeply troubled by the whole experience.

"What is it?" his wife asked, recognizing his distress.

"I warned him not to spread his message about Jesus, but he wouldn't listen. We seriously beat him. I can't believe I did that. I don't know if he's still alive or if we beat him to death."

"You need to go check on him," she urged.

Her husband took her suggestion and soon did the unthinkable: climbing into the pit to retrieve Suta, then carrying him to the safety of his own home. There, he and his wife nursed his former enemy back to health and released him when they were sure he could manage on his own.

"If God is real, he will watch over him," the man told his wife.

But four days later, Suta again returned to the village. And this time, both the man and his wife listened to his gospel message. Today, Suta pastors a church there, and his former persecutor has become his parishioner.

"When you pray for the persecuted, please remember to also pray for those who persecute," said the man who was once so furious at Suta for his willingness to sacrifice all for the sake of the gospel. "For us, it may be the only way we will see the love of God."

AN ACCEPTABLE SACRIFICE

The Bible itself provides the best commentary on the Bible. When we have trouble understanding or interpreting a passage, we must look to the whole body of Scripture to find the help we seek.

Such is the case with the story of Cain and Abel in Genesis 4. Behind the first murder in the Bible lies a backstory that some see as pointing to an unjust God. Why would he accept Abel's sacrifice and not Cain's? Was he showing some sort of favoritism? Did God prefer meat (Abel's offering) to vegetables (Cain's)?

We might subscribe to either or both of the above theories if we failed to look at the full counsel of Scripture. Early in Hebrews 11 lies a verse that provides the clarity we need: "By faith Abel offered to God a more acceptable sacrifice than Cain, through which he was commended as righteous, God commending him by accepting his gifts. And through his faith, though he died, he still speaks" (Hebrews 11:4).

In accepting Abel's offering, God received a pure sacrifice that displayed Abel's *faith*. The verse in Hebrews brings clarity to what we see in Genesis 4. With his gift ("an offering of the fruit of the ground," v. 3), Cain revealed the lack of faith in his heart by meeting the outward requirement, yet only offering the bare minimum. He gave the ordinary rather than the ideal.

Abel's offering ("of the firstborn of the flock and of their fat portions," v. 4) also revealed his heart. Again, if we look further into the Bible, we see those offerings of the firstborn or firstfruits received special honor (Exodus 13:2, 11–15; 34:22, 26). Abel offered his best; Cain's lack of faith sought the minimum requirements, no more.

As we learn in 1 Samuel 16:7, God looks beyond the external or superficial. Rather than seeing and comparing the two offerings, he saw and compared the two hearts. Abel's heart revealed his powerful faith and trust in God, while Cain's showed only his desire to check boxes on an imaginary spiritual scorecard.

Ultimately, God did not care about the quality of the gifts as much as the quality of faith they represented. For this reason, he did not accept Cain's offering, and for this reason, Abel's faith—not his brother's—receives honor in Hebrews 11:4.

The tragic turn of this story, Cain killing his brother and receiving a curse rather than a blessing from God, further reveals his lack of faith. He did not trust that God "rewards those who seek him" (Hebrews 11:6), so he took matters into his own hands, soon to be stained with his brother's blood.

In examining our own lives, we must also consider Scripture's guidance and offer the sacrifices most pleasing to God. As with Cain, Polycarp, Suta, and millions of faithful believers through the centuries, these will always include the best, most faith-filled offerings from pure and grace-filled hearts, and the quiet surrender of lives fully devoted to the Lord.

SUFFERING GREATLY—PRAISING THE LORD

Jesus warns his disciples, "They will also persecute you" (John 15:20). Fifteen Roman emperors used torture to intimidate believers in an attempt to eradicate the Christian faith from the world. Tender maidens and children received atrocious treatment.

Agnes and Priscilla, both thirteen years old, were torn by metal hooks, roasted on grills, and crowned with red-hot helmets. Millions of Christians were slain in the fourth century under the persecution directed by Diocletian in the Roman empire.

However, the magnitude of the slaughter did not cause the surviving Christians to panic. Amidst the torment, they retained their joy and their calm. Augustine wrote, "Every one of them seemed to be two people—one, somebody who suffers greatly, and also somebody who speaks words of gladness, of wisdom, and of praising the Lord." This is why, in the words of the early church leader, Tertullian, the blood of the martyrs became the seed of the church. It caused the church to grow.

No Christian is alone during tribulation. Sacrificial living does not result in a solitary confinement from the presence of God. That presence leaves no one without comfort.

Just before Betty and John Stam were captured to face martyrdom at the hands of Communist soldiers in China's Anwhei province, John Stam wrote to his father: "We're now in dangerous territory, but we're not afraid. The enclosed poem exactly expresses our feelings." E.H. Hamilton wrote the poem after he was inspired by the courage of Jack Vinson, the first Southern Presbyterian martyr in China:

Afraid? Of What?
To feel the spirit's glad release?
To pass from pain to perfect peace,
The strife and strain of life to cease?
    Afraid—of that?
    Afraid—of What?
Afraid to see the Savior's face
To hear His welcome, and to trace
The glory gleam from wounds of grace?
    Afraid—of that?
    Afraid—of What?
A flash, a crash, a pierced heart;
Darkness, light, O, Heaven's art!
A wound of His a counterpart!
    Afraid—of that?

Afraid—of What?
To do by death what life could not—
Baptize with blood a stony plot,
Till souls shall blossom from the spot?
Afraid of that?[1]

All biblical disciples who embrace a life of sacrificial living will experience persecution, yet their faith is buoyed by the presence of Christ.

DYING TO LIVE

Jesus gave us the supreme example of self-sacrifice through the painful death he suffered on the cross, giving his life for the sins of all people. But he also pointed his followers to the necessity of the sacrificial life with commands that included the following: "If anyone would come after me, let him deny himself and take up his cross and follow me. For whoever would save his life will lose it, but whoever loses his life for my sake will find it" (Matthew 16:24–25; see also Luke 9:23).

Jesus was not referring to the occasional self-denial we practice with our fading annual goals or intentions to improve ourselves through more frequent Bible reading. His words instead defined the true nature of discipleship: offering ourselves in full surrender to Christ with a continuing commitment to obey his will. Taking up our cross means facing certain death to ourself, our desires, and our motives, regardless of the physical death we may also face as a result. It means trusting the power of Christ's resurrection above all else for all situations, in life and in death. It means choosing a sacrificial life over a self-centered one.

Paul, in both his life and his New Testament letters, also pointed to the necessity of self-sacrifice. We find what are arguably his most poignant words on the topic buried in his little letter to the Philippians, where he wrote:

> Have this mind among yourselves, which is yours in Christ Jesus, who, though he was in the form of God, did not count equality with God a thing to be grasped, but emptied himself, by taking the form of a servant, being born in the likeness of men. And being found in human form, he humbled himself by becoming obedient to the point of death, even death on a cross (Philippians 2:5–8).

Here, Paul calls us to set aside our tendency to cling to worldly power and use the indwelling power of the mind of Christ to embrace the role of a servant. He highlights the choice Jesus made to humble himself, giving us both exemplar and hope for the choices we make toward a life that can be, as Paul described, "a living sacrifice" (Romans 12:1).

SAYING YES TO JESUS

"Once I said yes to Jesus, I was committed. I was all in."

John Allen Chau sent these words via video to a church supporting his missionary work. They describe not only the decision that ultimately led to his death, but also all the decisions, small and large, that preceded it. His nearly decade-long journey of preparation to reach a remote tribe on North Sentinel Island (a protected area of India) began in 2008, the year he turned seventeen. He became, in his words, "an apprentice to Jesus."

After taking his first missions trip the following year, he began to pray about spending his life serving God as a missionary. John asked God where he wanted him to go, echoing the prophet Isaiah's affirmation, "Here I am! Send me" (Isaiah 6:8). When he found information online about the Sentinelese people, whose isolated location in the Bay of Bengal had kept them from hearing the gospel, John sensed God's call to travel to North Sentinel Island and share God's love.

That's when he said yes to Jesus—and that's when his physical, emotional, and spiritual preparation began. Every decision he made as he got ready became part of the foundation God laid for John to live among the Sentinelese and share the gospel with them.

"He had conditioned his body, his mind, his spirit," said a missions leader who had mentored John during his college years. "He was one of the most prepared men I've ever met." Using everything from regular cold showers (to help his body adapt to living without hot water) to a series of immunizations (so he wouldn't infect the Sentinelese with imported diseases) to linguistic and medical training, John demonstrated his passion for the people he longed to reach.

In fact, he remained so focused on his future that he sometimes needed reminders to keep serving in the here and now. After a challenge from a mentor in college, John became involved with a soccer ministry for immigrants from Myanmar and also served with an after-school ministry in a low-income, high-crime area of his hometown. In both ministries, he served in whatever way was needed, without highlighting his service or seeking accolades.

"John had a unique way of making people feel seen, valued, and loved," said a classmate. "After talking to John, I'd get in my car and I'd pray, 'God, make me more like John.'"

The missions agency that had overseen one of John's college mission trips also helped him in the preparation process for North Sentinel Island. They offered books, counsel, and other support while John took four scouting trips to the Andaman Islands to learn more about the area and confirm God's call. Every trip affirmed what God had shown him: no one was trying to reach the Sentinelese with the gospel.

"I had been doubting a bit," John told a supporting church in a video he made about his first Andaman visit. "God, have you *really* told me to go here? Is this *really* where I'm supposed to be? Isn't there someone that you've called that's from here, that you're raising up to reach this people group?"

God continued to confirm John's call, and John continued his planning and preparation. He wrote plans for the first day, for his early goals, and even a contingency plan in case things didn't go well. Either way, he remained at peace. He had committed his life to seeing the Sentinelese people worship Jesus Christ as their Savior. He would either live on the island as a guest and a light for Christ, or he would give his life on the island and enter eternity.

History now records that John needed his contingency plan. Boarding a fishing boat and then taking a kayak to reach the island, both of his initial contacts with the Sentinelese ended with threats of violence. During his second attempt, a young Sentinelese launched an arrow that lodged firmly in John's waterproof Bible. Next, islanders moved between him and his kayak, forcing him to leave it—with his U.S. passport inside—and swim back to the boat.

The next day, November 26, 2018, John went ashore on North Sentinel Island for the final time. When the fishing boat returned a day later, according to the police report, the crew saw "a dead person being buried at the shore, which from the silhouette of the body, clothing, and circumstances appeared to be the body of John Allen Chau."

In one of his last journal entries, John wrote, "The eternal lives of this tribe are at hand, and I can't wait to see them around the throne of God worshiping in their own language, as Revelation 7:9–10 states."

Although his obedience to that focus ultimately led to his death, John Chau's journey was marked by the daily decisions of a sacrificial life long before that life ended on the shores of North Sentinel Island.

A prayer written in his journal on the night before he died reflected the commitment to self-sacrifice that built within him a heroic faith: "Whoever comes after me, whether it's tomorrow or another time, please give them a double anointing and bless them mightily."

"I WILL DO WHAT I MUST DO"

The testimony of another man named John also demonstrates a commitment to living a sacrificial life for the glory of God. Residing and working in the Southeast Asian nation of Myanmar, which is one of the world's most dangerous and difficult mission frontiers, Brother John lives boldly for Christ—and pays a great price.

But he didn't start out with such an unshakable commitment. An indigenous mission leader from a minority people group who were cannibals just three generations ago, Brother John said he had never wanted to become a minister. "In 1997 . . . the Lord turned my life upside down, and I committed myself to the Lord to involve [myself] in full-time ministry."

Following that, he spent some time in India, where he visited Reverend Nelson Numa, whom he knew to be a man of God. Brother John asked the reverend to pray for him, which resulted in a life-changing invitation to live in the pastor's home for a time. Brother John accepted, and when he left to return to Myanmar, Nelson gave him a book as a special gift.

Back in his own home, Brother John pulled out the book one evening. "When I finished reading that book, I was on my knees with tears, asking the Lord what was his will for my life," he explained.

"My perspective and now my worldview and now my vision, everything is changed, and my Christian life is completely changed. And I think this book is one of the best books I have ever read. … Every Christian should read this book."

What book spoke to Brother John in such a profound way? *Tortured for Christ* by Richard Wurmbrand, the story of the torture, imprisonment, and other Communist persecution he faced while living out a life of faith in Bucharest, Romania. "When he [spent] fourteen long years in prison, he never renounced his faith—still very faithful to the Lord," Brother John said. "And it was amazing to know his story, that he loved his enemy very much."

Despite government regulations in support of religious freedom in Myanmar, Brother John said persecution there is increasing. "The Buddhist monks in the local community are becoming more radical because they believe that if the government is giving more freedom to other religions, especially, they believe that Christianity will grow very rapidly," he explained.

He and his fellow Christians encounter persecution in the form of constant military checkpoints, even when traveling within their home city. They must register overnight guests with local government officials, giving their name, identification number, and the reason for the visit. Majority religious leaders incite the community to burn churches. Pastors and church leaders are imprisoned, and their activities are constantly monitored. But Brother John's long-ago prayer toward a sacrificial life, one in which he offered himself to God as a martyr "if I am counted worthy," remains a constant that continues to empower him.

"Yes, the oppression we face from the government is constant and difficult, but I know that everything that I experience has filtered through the hands of God," he said.

Brother John was leading a team of missionaries in one region of the country, when, each time he visited to encourage and bring resources, the local officials would harass him by calling him to the government office. After the seventh time he was called into the office and threatened, Brother John looked directly at the official in charge and said, "I am going to continue to do what I do no matter what. You do what you must do, and I will do what I must do."

His steadfast commitment to follow Christ at any cost and speak truth to power caused the official to back off, but Brother John continues to experience much opposition in his ministry. Still, he sees nothing unusual about his commitment to a sacrificial life.

"Becoming a true Christian doesn't happen just by good preaching and anything but when the Holy Spirit touched their heart and changed their life, then they become a true Christian. And whoever becomes a true Christian, and whoever met Jesus personally—most of the people that I have met in our mission field, and also among our new believers . . . every one of them is willing to pay the price of following Jesus Christ, whatever the cost is."

FOR REFLECTION AND DISCUSSION:

1. What comes to mind when you hear the word *sacrifice*? What about *sacrificial living?*
2. Describe someone you know whose life points to self-sacrifice for the cause of Christ.
3. How did Suta's willingness to sacrifice impact the life of his persecutor? How does it impact you?
4. John Chau's story was told and retold around the world, often with a critical eye from the secular media. What new truths about his story did you learn in this chapter?

5. Which chapter story—biblical, historical, or modern—spoke to you most about the value of sacrificial living? How will it impact the choices you make today?
6. When studying Scripture, we must pay attention to its context. Read Matthew 16:21–28. Why do you think Jesus spoke about the need to die to ourselves and pick up our cross immediately after his rebuke of Peter for denying the necessity of Jesus' coming death and resurrection? In what areas is God calling you to die to yourself?

Visit vom.org/HeroicFaith to view Suta's story along with additional brief feature videos and digital resources.

HEROIC FAITH

CHAPTER 5

EMBRACE TRUE COURAGE

"I am not alone. I am with Christ, who walked this path for me. And this gives me the courage to go on."

—Sarah, China

Courageous. Loyal. Steadfast.

These adjectives describe the men of the Theban Legion, a group of 6,600 Christians from Thebes in Upper Egypt who were recruited and trained for the Imperial Roman army in the third century A.D. What marked them more than their military expertise was their heroic faith—a faith that ultimately gave them the courage to stand for Christ above even their commitment to their ruler.

History records that Emperor Maximian ordered these brave soldiers, commanded by Mauritius, to march west over the Alps to help quell an insurrection in Gaul. A long march preceded a brief military campaign and victory. Maximian, like most other emperors, was a man of immense self-importance. Wanting to celebrate the victory, he ordered his troops to take the Oath of Allegiance—which stated that Maximian was divine—and then to help exterminate all Christians remaining in the Burgandy region.

Mauritius replied that because his own men were Christian, he would withdraw from the main encampment. He and his men could not kill innocents without dishonoring the oath they had taken at baptism to love and serve God above all else.

This response from a legion commander insulted the emperor, who replied with an order of decimation: every tenth man in the Theban Legion was to be executed.

And so it was done; 660 warriors were killed.

Despite their losses, the Legion could neither take the Oath of Allegiance nor draw swords against brothers of faith. Maximian ordered a second decimation; another 600 soldiers were slaughtered.

The survivors had choices to make. Would they defend themselves? Comply with the order? Await another massacre? Mauritius and his lieutenants replied to Maximian with as clear a statement of loyalty as any soldier could offer:

> Emperor, we are your soldiers but also the soldiers of the true God. We owe you military service and obedience, but we cannot renounce him who is our Creator and Master—and also yours even though you reject him. In all things that are not against his law, we most willingly obey you, as we have done hitherto. We readily oppose your enemies, whoever they are, but we cannot stain our hands with the blood of innocent people (Christians). We have taken an oath to God before we took one to you. You cannot place any confidence in our second oath if we violate the other (the first). You commanded us to execute Christians; behold we are such. We confess God the Father, the creator of all things, and his Son Jesus Christ. We have seen our comrades slain with the sword. We do not

> weep for them but rather rejoice at their honor. Neither this nor any other provocation has tempted us to revolt. Behold, we have arms in our hands, but we do not resist, because we would rather die innocent than live by any sin.

Rather than responding with pride in their courage and delight in their resolve to defend his empire, Maximian became enraged and condemned them all to death. The Legion did not attempt to muster a defense or find a hiding place, and those posted away from the encampment did not run. Nearly six thousand battle-hardened troops were killed for their first allegiance to Christ by their second-in-command, Emperor Maximian, on September 22, 286.

The story of the Theban Legion reveals both heroic faith and the kind of courage that can only come as its fruit. As we follow Christ, the qualities he builds within us develop a more heroic faith in our lives. We become more like Jesus and, as a result, are filled with the kind of faith, love, and power he exhibited when he walked among us.

That heroic faith also bears visible fruit in our lives, fruit we easily recognize as marking the faithfulness of Christians throughout the centuries.

COURAGE TO SURRENDER

Hebrews 11 brings us a picture of courage as a fruit of faith in verse 23: "By faith Moses, when he was born, was hidden for three months by his parents, because they saw that the child was beautiful, and they were not afraid of the king's edict." Although Moses is named here, it is not his faith that challenges us but that of his parents, which laid the foundation for Moses later embracing the one true God.

The Bible teaches us to submit to our authorities, but those of heroic faith understand that when an order from an earthly authority contradicts God's mandate, we must obey God rather than man. As a refugee in Persia (modern-day Iran), Daniel demonstrated this principle, maintaining his habit of praying to God three times a day despite the decree from King Darius that no one should pray to anyone except him (Daniel 6:6–10).

Moses' parents, Amram and Jochebed, courageously defied the king's edict. The rationale for their decision, however, reveals itself in the words placed—most likely for emphasis—at the end of the verse: "they were not afraid of the king's edict (Hebrews 11:23)." That statement is significant, because parents who disobeyed that command by keeping their sons alive would be destroyed. Amram and Jochebed were risking their son's life by sending him down the river in a simple basket boat and placing their own lives in danger; they trusted in God's power to save their son more than they trusted in the king.

As with the doomed but stalwart men of the Theban Legion, the heroic faith of Moses' parents bore the fruit of courage. That courage gave the couple the push it must have taken to send their little one floating down a crocodile-infested river with only a young girl—the baby's sister, Miriam—to watch over him from a distance. God had promised to deliver the Israelites from their slavery in Egypt, and these parents trusted God to fulfill that promise despite the king's decree.

But Amram and Jochebed's courage did not end here. God's plan for Moses included Pharaoh's daughter finding the baby in his river-borne basket, adopting him and—following a divinely appointed season where she employed Jochebed as his nurse—raising him in Pharaoh's palace, never to return to the home of his birth. Surrendering their child to become part of Pharaoh's household likely required even greater courage of Moses' parents than constructing the reed basket or watching it float away with the three-month-old infant inside.

Such a decision, as well as such courage, rises only from a heroic faith in God.

COURAGE TO STAND FIRM

The same kind of heroic faith bore abundant fruit in the life of Sarah, a young editor for an illegal, underground Chinese newspaper, until officials from the Chinese Communist Party decided to punish her. They considered her a criminal and came to her home one night to arrest her.

"I knew the risks of what I was doing, but I wasn't prepared for what I would go through that night," Sarah said. Although she had often read the Bible's repeated encouragement, "Do not fear," she was fearful as soldiers dragged her, still in her pajamas, to a waiting truck with no explanation.

"I have been arrested before, but this is not an arrest, and I am not being brought to the police station," she recalled. "I quickly realize they have more than questions for me." After the soldiers dumped her out of the truck, guards dragged her into a cell, slamming the door behind her.

"I felt so alone," she said of that night. "All I could hear is my heartbeat, and with every beat, the sound grew louder, and I became more afraid."

More shouts. More beatings. Soon, a man in uniform brandished a document before her face—one the officials wanted her to sign, confessing her so-called crimes and making a statement against her friends. Refusing, Sarah prayed the night would pass quickly as the men yelled, pushed, and further threatened her before leaving her cell.

Then one of her captors returned. After Sarah again refused to sign the paper, he pressed a lit cigarette into the palm of her hand as she screamed in pain.

More torture followed, with more unbearable pain, moving Sarah to consider the unthinkable: *Would signing the document be so wrong? And if it was, wouldn't God forgive me?*

The torture continued. Next, guards placed chains on her legs, forcing her to walk back and forth throughout the night, crying out to God for strength in her suffering and wishing she had signed the document after all.

"Hours have passed when I notice the footprints on the floor," Sarah said. "They are my footprints, and they have been made from walking in the trail of my own blood."

Rather than crushing her, the sight of those bloody footprints spurred Sarah on.

"I think of Christ and of how he was beaten before walking to Golgotha, how he must have also left a trail of his own blood," she said. "He also was hated by this world. In a small way, I now suffer for him. I am not alone. I am with Christ, who walked this path for me. And this gives me the courage to go on."

And she needed that courage. Sarah then endured six months in a labor camp, making Christmas lights.

Sarah never signed the document, and she never betrayed her friends or her Lord. May her story inspire our hearts to pursue a more heroic faith—and the heart of courage it yields.

COURAGE WHERE BOMBS FALL

When you minister in a war zone, courage becomes a moment-by-moment necessity. Such is the case for David, Maria, and their three sons, who live in an area of Colombia known for drug trafficking and violence between two Marxist groups.

Shortly after the family moved to a town of more than forty thousand people, David and Maria realized the danger surrounding their new home. As their nine-year-old son returned from a shopping errand for his mother, two stray bullets from guerrilla gunfire struck him in the neck—one missing a major artery by only one millimeter. After fully recovering, the boy helped lead worship with his two brothers at one of the three churches his family planted.

The family has also received anonymous threats. A few years ago, someone slipped a note under their front door, warning them to leave within twenty-four hours or be killed. "I'll never forget how Maria turned pale when she picked up the note and read it," David said.

Despite the threats, the couple decided to continue their ministry. But before long, they faced a new level of danger. Two guerrilla groups engaged in battle near the Arauca River, which forms the border between Colombia and Venezuela. Bombs dropping on enemy locations regularly rattled David and Maria's church.

"You hear the bombs every night, the gunfire every night," Maria said. "You are in the service preaching, and the building shakes because of the bombs."

Despite the trauma of the constant bombing, their congregation faithfully fed and cared for many of the five thousand Venezuelans displaced by the conflict, using the devastation as a bridge for evangelism.

"It has been a good way to share the gospel," David said, smiling. "We have been able to give glory to God, because I have seen

God back me up, taking care of us in every moment and in all situations."

David and Maria's heroic faith has given birth not only to a passion for souls, but also to the courage it takes to reach them for Christ amid dire circumstances. "Everything has to do with the calling of the Lord and knowing that it's God's will," David said. "I see it every day in how he backs me up. God called me to that place."

COURAGE TO FACE DEATH

Even for those who have fully surrendered to Christ, facing danger and possible death takes a special kind of courage. Warren and Donna Pett had the kind of faith that birthed courage, and their children knew it. When the couple sold their long-held family farm and traveled to the mission field to share the gospel as they taught agriculture to African youth, they did so in faith, not fear.

"Our parents were absolutely certain of where they were going when they died," said their son Saul. "Because of that certainty, they were willing to go wherever they felt they were called to go. If you had told them before they left that leaving would cost them their lives in service of their Lord, they still would have gone. It wouldn't have changed their minds. It might have changed how they said goodbye, but nothing was stopping them."

It didn't take long for the potential dangers of their mission to surface. A civil war in the Democratic Republic of the Congo led them to cancel their plans for agricultural ministry and take administrative roles in Nairobi, Kenya, instead. But as soon as a position opened for teaching agriculture, they moved to northwestern Uganda to fulfill what they saw as their true calling.

"As they were leaving, pieces just fell into place, so it felt very God-centered as they were doing it," Saul said. "They definitely saw God's hand in the whole thing as it was happening."

A local Muslim elder in the Yumbe district, a majority-Muslim area, had donated more than one thousand acres to establish a school among the Aringa people group, which is 89% Muslim. The school promoted spiritual growth through leadership development, biblical training, and evangelistic outreach while teaching skills in such areas as agriculture, carpentry, and computers. A sponsoring ministry built the school near the edge of the donated land, and the Petts, other staff members, and students lived in temporary mud huts with thatched roofs while awaiting permanent housing. The remainder of the land was to be farmed in service to the community.

Those in the community, however, weren't entirely welcoming of Christians. Tensions between Muslims and Christians had increased as a result of the U.S.-Iraq conflict, with fanatical Muslims viewing the war as an assault on all Muslims by Christians. Prior to the Petts' arrival at the school, two missionary couples were attacked.

Sometime after Warren and Donna started teaching, the ministry's director received threatening letters from local Islamic leaders, ordering him to shut down the school. But a missionary who had become the Petts' close friend said Warren wasn't afraid. "I think he knew why he was there and that he was called. He wasn't going to be shaken by these threats."

And the threats were real. On the night of March 18, 2004, the Petts had retired to their hut when two armed men—faces covered and wearing military fatigues—entered the school area, threatening both the director, Anyandru "Elly" Moses, and another staff member. Several students rushed to the Petts' hut to warn them but received no response. Warren had opened the door to their hut after hearing shots that killed one of the students. Gunmen ordered him and Donna to come outside and kneel side by side. The two men shot them to death.

Even now, the Petts' courage inspires others. Although the school has since closed for financial reasons, "the vision remains to use the land and resources to further advance the gospel among the Aringa people," Elly said. Today, he and others continue their efforts to reach Muslim communities with the gospel.

"Their deaths inspired us not to fear Islam but to confront all the lies with boldness," he said. "From a physical perspective, that was the end; but from a spiritual perspective, it was the beginning of the battle."

The Petts' children also find inspiration in remembering their parents' courage and in the continuing gospel work in Uganda. Sons Saul and Ezra visited the country for the first time in 2022. With Elly as their guide, the two men visited the place where their parents were martyred and learned that, even so long after the attack, many in Yumbe still remember and mourn the deaths of Warren and Donna.

Inspired by "warriors of faith" who turned their grief and anger into a commitment to advancing God's kingdom in a place hostile to the gospel, Saul and Ezra said they witnessed a depth of faith they had never experienced.

It was too late for the Petts to muster up courage when they were ordered to kneel before their killers. That quality had already been birthed in their hearts through the heroic faith they built by a lifetime of daily decisions to follow Christ. Their discipleship journey allowed them to hear and recognize God's voice and obey his instruction while trusting he would guide their journey—even when it ended in death.

COURAGE TO FIGHT

The heroic faith of the Old Testament's King Hezekiah also bore the fruit of courage—a courage that strengthened both him and the people he ruled in the kingdom of Judah. As part of his broad campaign to conquer the region, Assyrian King Sennacherib and his army advanced toward Jerusalem.

In this time of crisis, Hezekiah could have turned to any number of avenues for assistance, including a potential alliance with the powerful kingdom of Egypt. Instead, he set about preparing Jerusalem for attack by rebuilding the broken city wall, repairing various areas, and making weapons and shields. He did not ignore the looming violence in any way.

But he also did something much more important. After organizing his people under military captains, Hezekiah gathered them and instructed, "Do not be afraid or dismayed before the king of Assyria and all the horde that is with him, for there are more with us than with him" (2 Chronicles 32:7).

Hezekiah's heroic faith moved him into the spectacular understanding that his people's defense must not rest on their physical preparation but on their strength, courage, and persistence in the face of what appeared would be certain defeat. Like Elisha, who saw by faith the hills full of chariots and fire that his servant could not see at first (2 Kings 10:15–17), he rested in the confidence of greater numbers and immutable strength. In fact, he quoted Elisha in this passage when he said, "There are more with us than with him" (2 Kings 6:16).

Hezekiah explains what he means in 2 Chronicles 32:8: "'With him is an arm of flesh, but with us is the Lord our God, to help us and to fight our battles.' And the people took confidence from the words of Hezekiah king of Judah."

Despite Sennacherib's attempts to discredit Hezekiah and discourage the people of Judah who were in Jerusalem (vv. 9–19), Hezekiah and Isaiah the prophet called on the God of heaven (v. 20). And just as God was with Elisha and the angelic army surrounding him and his servant, God was also with Hezekiah and his people, striking down the entire Assyrian army that numbered 185,000 (2 Chronicles 32:21–22, 2 Kings 19:35).

As we have seen, a heroic faith bears the fruit of courage that defies any other explanation than the supernatural power of God—a power he perfects in our weakness (2 Corinthians 12:9). No matter what situation we face, we can cling to the truth both Elisha and Hezekiah proclaimed: "There are more with us than with [them]."

COURAGE—A GIFT OF GOD

Arrested at the age of twenty-one for belonging to a patriotic organization, Gheorge Calciu, a Romanian underground priest, had a warm brotherly relationship with persecuted Protestants. Richard Wurmbrand was in prison with him.

Gheorge suffered the worst torture. He was forced to eat his own excrement and drink his own urine. One could escape these atrocities by claiming to have been re-educated in Communist ideology and proving it by torturing one's friends.

Gheorge cracked under the pressure, but he received grace from God and was converted. After he was released during a general amnesty, he was forbidden to study theology to become a priest; therefore, he did so secretly. He became an Orthodox priest and a heroic one. All his fear was gone. From great depths of sin, he rebounded to the heights of holiness.

In 1978, Gheorge announced he would preach a series of seven Wednesday sermons, which confronted Romanian dictator Nicolae Ceausescu's treatment of Christians. Seminary students and other young people flocked to hear him preach. After his third sermon, Communists locked the door of the church to prevent students from attending. Officials then locked the gate to the seminary, so the students jumped over the walls to hear the priest. Gheorge was warned that priests in Communist countries must be on the side of the atheists in power, but still he protested the demolition of Orthodox churches in Bucharest and the provincial towns.

He continued his stand despite threats of detention in an asylum. He was arrested again and sent back to prison. This time, officials treated him much worse. Still, Gheorge refused to relent, so the government decided to have cellmates kill him, but they refused. He was later exiled to the United States, where he died in 2006.

Gheorge valued courage, the rare gift of God, like a precious stone. From his story we see a man who had sinned yet grew in his own heroic faith.

COURAGE IN THE BATTLE

If missionaries could choose their assignments, one of the last places they would likely select is the town of Gashua, in Yobe state, Nigeria. Summer temperatures hover around 120 degrees, clouds of mosquitoes hang in the air, the drinking water carries various diseases, and a powdery dust causes chronic eye and respiratory problems. If that weren't enough, Yobe state is ravaged by ongoing violence from local Islamist groups.

"If I had my own wish, I would not go to Gashua," Pastor Elijah Ogunyi said. Like Jonah, Elijah at first resisted, but he knew the

Lord had been leading him toward a particular calling since childhood. "God had to cut my wings," Elijah said. "That is how I became a pastor."

A shoulder injury moved Elijah off the path that his polygamous family had set before him—becoming a witch doctor, just like his grandfather. Since he could no longer lift the heavy stone idols, his half-brother was assigned the ritual of sacrificing to the family gods. This freed Elijah to break family tradition by moving away after he came of age, avoiding polygamy and stopping the worship of idols. He traveled throughout Nigeria, using his training as an electrician to support himself. By the early 1990s, he married and settled in the central Nigerian city of Jos.

But God had other plans for this young man. Through a series of frightening dreams that included a Bible Elijah used to slay a dark figure, God moved him to surrender his life to Christ. After that, through another series of circumstances, he learned more about obedience—and despite the need to support his wife, Felicia, and five children, made the choice to attend seminary. When he completed that training, he expected to continue serving at his church. But once again, God had other plans.

God sent Elijah straight into the heart of territory controlled by the Islamist group, Boko Haram. The group had wreaked havoc in this part of northern Nigeria for about fifteen years. At the time Elijah served there, Boko Haram, which had pledged allegiance to the self-proclaimed Islamic State (ISIS), carried out almost daily attacks on Christians and government entities.

Elijah ended up in the town of Gashua in the Sahara Desert near the border with Niger, 250 miles from his family's home in Jos. Elijah, Felicia, and their youngest son moved to Gashua, leaving their other children with adult siblings in Jos so they could continue their education. "Daddy, are you leaving us?" Elijah's second daughter asked him.

"Yes, we will leave . . . If God wants me to leave, I will," he said.

In Gashua, Elijah and his family served at a church that, after a large-scale Boko Haram attack, had dwindled to only five men, three women, and five young people. "After the church was attacked, the people locked up the place and ran away," Elijah said. He has worked to build relationships with local young people who are at risk because of the region's extreme poverty and are targeted for recruitment by local Islamists.

The area, which is 99% Muslim, is increasingly hostile to Christians. Although Elijah has won the friendship of many Muslim neighbors, his church has been burglarized twice. "I have forgiven all those who persecute me because God teaches us to forgive," he said. "If I see them, I will share the gospel with them."

Still, with the terrorists looming, the threat of persecution remains. "We are afraid . . . because we know they will look for pastors first," Elijah explained. "Persecution is a part of the Christian life. If truly we pastors are called by God, we should expect persecution."

Because of the serious decline in Felicia's health, she and Elijah have again made Jos their home base. But the two remain committed to their work in Gashua, so Elijah travels back and forth—six hours each way—over potholed and dangerous roads, to maintain their ministry there.

Elijah summarized their bold stance, and that of many others of heroic faith, with these words: "We have made up our minds that it is better to die in battle for God than to die as a coward."

Lord, grant us such faith—and the courage it yields.

FOR REFLECTION AND DISCUSSION:

1. The Petts' adult children said, "Because of that certainty [going to heaven], they were willing to go wherever they felt they were called to go. If you had told them before they left that leaving would cost them their lives in service of their Lord, they still would have gone. It wouldn't have changed their minds. It might have changed how they said goodbye, but nothing was stopping them." As you reflect on the Petts' actions and the perspective of their children, how would you define courage?
2. How does the courage that comes from heroic faith differ from the courage of those without faith? Provide examples if you can.
3. Do you think the faith and resultant courage of Moses' parents influenced him later in life? If so, how so? If not, why not?
4. Seeing her own bloody footprints on the floor of her jail cell impacted Sarah in a powerful way. How did they move you as you watched the video? How do you think they will do so going forward?
5. How do you embrace a renewed sense of courage after failure? What about Gheorge Calciu's courage inspires you to live a more heroic faith?
6. Which of the stories in this chapter spoke most personally to you, and why? Take time to pray and ask God to give you a more heroic faith along with the fruit of courage.

Visit vom.org/HeroicFaith to view Sarah's story along with additional brief feature videos and digital resources.

HEROIC FAITH

CHAPTER 6

FAITHFUL ENDURANCE

"Persecution? Oh yes, of course, it is part of our faith. It is what the Bible says; we will face persecution from those that do not like us. We must be patient through this."

—MaLai Wan (Laos), facing threats from her village leaders for following Christ

How many of us would be willing to endure verbal assault, torture, even death? And how many of us would have had the strength to do so as a new Christian?

A Roman soldier named Alban gives us an example of endurance. In the fourth century A.D., emperor Diocletian published an edict against Christians, ordering churches to be burned to the ground and the Scriptures destroyed by fire. Alban, then a pagan, provided shelter for a Christian priest who was fleeing the authorities. The pastor's lifestyle and devotion, along with their many spiritual conversations, moved Alban both to faith in Christ and baptism.

But when the local magistrate sent soldiers to search for and arrest the missing priest, Alban exchanged clothes with him. The soldiers soon arrested Alban, wearing the priest's hooded cloak, and brought him before the magistrate. When the magistrate realized his prisoner was Alban and not the priest, he became enraged at Alban's bold offering of himself in place of his guest.

The magistrate ordered Alban to be dragged to the pagan gods. The official commanded soldiers to inflict the same punishment on Alban as the priest would have received. In the face of this pronouncement, Alban declared, "I worship and adore the true and living God who created all things." Unafraid, he added that he would not obey the government's commands.

"Of what house and stock are you?" the magistrate then asked.

"What business is it of yours of what lineage I am born? If on the other hand you desire to hear the truth of my religion, know that I am now a Christian and devote myself to Christlike service."

Incensed, the official ordered Alban to be beaten, hoping he would recant. But Alban patiently endured the torment.

Recognizing his prisoner's determination to confess Christ, the magistrate ordered his beheading. Alban was taken from the town of Verulamium to the top of the hill across the river, where St. Alban's Cathedral in England now stands.

In the year 304, Alban became Britain's first martyr for Christ. The second was the executioner ordered to kill him. Upon hearing Alban's testimony, he became a Christian on the spot and refused to obey the order. The third was the priest, who after hearing that Alban had been arrested in his place, hurried to the courts to turn himself in and save Alban.

Three lives. One heroic faith. All enduring the worst the persecutors had to offer for the best God has to offer: a faith in Christ that not only gives us the hope of heaven but also empowers us to endure to the end.

ENDURANCE UNDER ATTACK

Her serene tone stood in contrast to her heartbreaking story.

"My name is Janette. I am a Christian, and I love Jesus with all my heart. I love my children, and I love the people of my country, the Central African Republic."

Janette's life changed in little more than an instant when violent Islamic extremists ambushed her village. "Guns started firing, and we started running as fast as we could into the bush. All the Christians in our village were killed or driven into hiding. I fled with my children. We didn't even have time to put on our shoes or clothes."

But Janette's story is far from unique. Tens of thousands of our Christian brothers and sisters in the Central African Republic have a similar experience. They live, sometimes for years, in makeshift, temporary shelters as the violence continues. Muslim rebels have targeted Christians to eliminate their bold faith in and witness to Christ.

Not only do Janette and her fellow believers love and forgive their persecutors, but they also endure the continuing persecution with the strength God alone can supply—trusting him to meet their needs despite danger, distress, and displacement. Because of the endurance their heroic faith produced, Christ remains their hope in life and death.

A GROWING ENDURANCE

Moses receives more attention in Hebrews 11 than any other faith hero, the author giving a brief summary of several key events in his life of pain and promise. How much influence did the faith of Moses' parents have on his life? We may never know the answer, but we see the same sort of courageous faith in their youngest child as we do in the lives of Amram and Jochebed (see Chapter 5 of this book and Hebrews 11:23). However, upon close examination, we also see the fruit of endurance, which rose from the kind of heroic faith whereby Moses defied the Egyptian Pharaoh. He took the people of God across the Red Sea, and led them for a generation in the wilderness journey.

Moses endured mistreatment (Hebrews 11:24–25). Rather than accepting the power and privilege of his royal position, he obeyed God's calling on his life and all the consequences that came with that obedience. And he did something we often find difficult today—counting the gift of suffering persecution for his confidence in God's plan as more valuable than money. In Moses' case, that included the trappings of the royal family's wealth ("the treasures of Egypt," v. 26). While his faith-born endurance by no means made his decision easy, it meant he could face these challenges with an eternal perspective rather than an earthly viewpoint.

But Moses' endurance had an even broader impact. There's no doubt he acted in anger when he took the life of the Egyptian task-master (Exodus 2:12–15). But Hebrews 11:27 tells us his departure from Egypt came as the result of his faith. Though fallible, his eternal perspective allowed him to see "him who is invisible" and make that and future decisions on the basis of faith, not fear, anger, or guilt over his sin. Moses held God as his ultimate authority rather than Pharaoh and his temporal, yet powerful, rule.

God used Moses' forty years in the desert of Midian to refine him for his return to his homeland to lead his people out of bondage. God spoke this command to Moses using a burning bush (Exodus 3:1–22). As Stephen recounted in his sermon to the Jewish tribunal known as the Sanhedrin, "This Moses, whom they rejected, saying,

'Who made you a ruler and a judge?'—this man God sent as both ruler and redeemer by the hand of the angel who appeared to him in the bush" (Act 7:35).

As we read his story in the Old Testament, we have the opportunity to see the faithful endurance of Moses grow in a way the quick summary in Hebrews 11 does not allow. He returned to Egypt as the called-out but reluctant leader. But after confronting Pharaoh multiple times as God sent plagues against Egypt, Moses was ready for a step that required even more faith: telling his people to trust God to protect their children even as the Egyptians' firstborn children are struck dead by God (Exodus 12:12).

Moses explained that God would pass over any house that had its doorposts and lintel painted with the blood of a sacrificial lamb. This, he told the Israelites, is "the sacrifice of the LORD's Passover" (Exodus 12:27). But as the author of Hebrews points out, it was "by faith" that Moses instructed the Hebrew people in observing Passover and the sprinkling of the blood. Only by seeing the steadfast faith of Moses could the Israelites have confidence that God would protect them from judgment. Moses' heroic faith influenced the Israelites to choose obedience, even when it didn't make sense to their human understanding.

Finally, the author of Hebrews tells us that "by faith the people crossed the Red Sea as on dry land, but the Egyptians, when they attempted to do the same, were drowned" (Hebrews 11:29). Neither the Israelites nor the Egyptians suffered from a lack of courage. Yet the Israelites' courage was founded on a steadfast faith in God.

As his people prepared to enter their unusual Red Sea pathway, Moses called them to faith: "Fear not, stand firm, and see the salvation of the LORD, which he will work for you today. For the Egyptians whom you see today, you shall never see again. The Lord will fight for you, and you have only to be silent" (Exodus 14:13–14).

Moses' faithful endurance translated to the most essential of leadership skills: leading his people to follow God as he did. Not only did he stretch out his arm over the water to open a pathway for the Israelites, but he took the next step of obedience, again stretching out his arm to send the sea rushing back over the Egyptians. The Israelites, operating by faith, passed through the sea "as on dry land" (Hebrews 11:29), but when the Egyptians sought to follow their example without that faith, they were drowned.

In the end, "Israel saw the great power that the Lord used against the Egyptians, so the people feared the Lord, and they believed in the Lord and in his servant Moses" (Exodus 14:31). The endurance that came as a result of Moses' heroic faith was now displayed in the people of Israel—a needed asset for their challenging forty-year sojourn in the wilderness.

ENDURANCE FOR PERSECUTION

"Mr. Xi," a Christian in China, lives a long way from the Red Sea. But when we look at this calm, soft-spoken man's faith and passion for the Lord, we see many similarities to Moses.

Mr. Xi's pharaoh is the Chinese Communist Party (CCP), which has persecuted him, as well as his father and grandfather before him. His grandfather, a house church pastor and missionary to other parts of China after Mao Zedong's 1949 Communist takeover, spent more than ten years in prison for his faith. Mr. Xi's father, a leader in the church, was detained by police on many occasions.

In the neighborhood where Mr. Xi grew up, there were only a handful of cars. So the few times a vehicle came down his street, it usually meant authorities were coming to arrest his father. When that happened, Mr. Xi's father would calmly ask his wife to collect some extra clothes for him in case his "visit" to the police station turned into weeks or months in prison.

Growing up with such an inspiring example, it's no surprise that Mr. Xi also is involved in gospel work. His firsthand understanding of the cost of ministering for Christ in China, coupled with his heroic faith, has yielded the fruit of endurance. He wasn't surprised or deterred when he was mistreated because of his bold witness. In fact, he sees benefits in persecution.

"Persecution is like fire," he said. "I use the word like *purify.* If we want pure gold, we have to let it go through fire." He said Christianity had become socially "cool" among Chinese people who considered it a Western religion and thought all Western culture was trendy.

"The blessing [of persecution] for the church is that when we are facing the difficulties, the serious believers will stay. So it doesn't matter what happens," Mr. Xi said. In other words, persecution leaves the church full of believers serious about their faith—serious enough that threats of arrest or physical pain can't keep them from meeting. Serious enough to endure. Those who are there only because it's "cool" quickly fall away. Churches full of pure, refined gold tend to be unstoppable.

Mr. Xi is one of those believers. Following in his family's footsteps, he's been detained by police on many occasions, and several times served fifteen days of "administrative detention." He used an unusual term to describe his first arrest: *privilege.*

Mr. Xi was enthused to proclaim that he was like his grandfather—imprisoned for the activity of his faith. Five years of Mr. Xi's prison time was in a province close to where his grandfather was imprisoned.

"I felt like I am so privileged in my family," he added. "Many years ago, my grandfather was here and suffered for the Lord, and today I am here. I just felt a privilege."

What Mr. Xi calls *privilege,* many of us would call *persecution.* And what he perceives as normal for the believer is what we might view as extraordinary endurance.

> I think Christianity is really a relationship, and God is real, and we have this relationship with him. And it is not just by saying, "Okay, God, we trust you." We trust him and know the Great Commission he has given us, so we are so honored to be his servants. I don't see any reason we shouldn't be happy. This is really a great blessing from him.
>
> By the way, you can save people. There are people in the prison, they are really hopeless people and they are facing a death sentence and they will be leaving [this] world [soon]. You have the chance to share the gospel with them and save their souls from death. What a blessing the first time I really experienced the miracle happening in that beautiful time.[1]

Mr. Xi has retained an attitude that persecution is a privilege beyond his initial visit to prison. He knows his current Bible distribution work could send him back there for three years or more. But his faith and the endurance it yielded have prepared him well.

"I mean, persecution and suffering, you can't really hide from it," he said. "If you are a real Christian, you will be persecuted. It doesn't matter—you will be persecuted if you want to be a godly person (2 Timothy 3:12).

"We all know if we choose to work for the Lord, sometime, maybe not now, you will be persecuted for sure."[2]

ENDURANCE IN MOURNING

When she talks about her husband, Justina often breaks down in tears. This young Nigerian mother's late husband, Nehemiah, was the victim of a militant Islamist Fulani attack. He and a friend traveled to a nearby village one day to baptize new believers who were part of their church.

Nehemiah never returned.

Instead, men from the neighboring village brought Justina his body. "I felt like dying," she recalled.

Fearing an attack on her village by the same militants who killed her husband, she and her young son stayed with her mother-in-law for a time after her husband's murder. Now, they have moved back to the home that reminds Justina of the loss of her husband every day.

Although she has continuing concerns that the violent attackers will return, Justina also has an endurance born of faith. "Losing my husband was the hardest thing, but God has given me the strength to bear the loss and to keep moving."

Justina still raises crops on the land her husband farmed about an hour's walk from her home, but she is careful to avoid potential danger. "When I hear that Fulani men are in the area, I stay home," she said. "I have never encountered them on the farm."

Despite the loss of her husband, killed because of his faithful obedience to Christ, Justina's words display her faithful endurance and long-term commitment to the Lord. "He (the Lord) has done everything for me," she said. "When I am sick, he heals me. When I pray, he answers. I see the evidence of all he does in my life. This is why I will not leave him."

RUNNING WITH ENDURANCE

While looking at so many examples of heroic faith from Hebrews 11, we can't overlook Hebrews 12, which effectively applies those examples by pointing to Jesus as the ultimate standard for biblical disciples. The first two verses in this chapter say: "Therefore, since we are surrounded by so great a cloud of witnesses, let us also lay aside every weight, and sin which clings so closely, and let us run with endurance the race that is set before us, looking to Jesus, the founder and perfecter of our faith, who for the joy that was set before him endured the cross, despising the shame, and is seated at the right hand of the throne of God."

Most modern Bibles translate *hupomone* (a Greek word, whose root words mean "under" and "abide") as "endurance." This interpretation gives weight to the idea of abiding or remaining under some form of discipline. It means living—in obedience to Christ—under even the most uncomfortable circumstances with our eyes on a greater goal. We are to "run with endurance" as Jesus "endured the cross."

The use of both "endurance" and "endured" in Hebrews 12 points to the significance of this quality for every believer. Regardless of what we face, we must endure—and our faith gives us the power to do so. While looking back at the life illustrations drawn for us in Hebrews 11, we can also look ahead, as Jesus did, to the joy set before us. We do so not with an attitude of something to suffer through, but with the triumphant certainty of victory that only a vibrant walk with Christ in faith brings.

We see this faithful endurance in the Old Testament biblical figures named in Hebrews 11, but we see it in New Testament figures as well. James, who urges us to "count it all joy" when we face trials, died at the hand of Herod Agrippa I (Acts 12:1–2). Stephen, chosen as one of the early church's first deacons, displayed an endurance anchored in his heroic faith when the Jews brought false witnesses against him. Throughout Stephen's defense before the high priest and subsequent stoning, Scripture tells us he "gazed into heaven and saw the glory of God, and Jesus standing at the right hand of God" (Acts 7:55).

And the apostle Paul who was used of God to display and demonstrate the endurance referred to in Hebrews 11 despite great suffering:

> Five times I received at the hands of the Jews the forty lashes less one. Three times I was beaten with rods. Once I was stoned. Three times I was shipwrecked; a night and a day I was adrift at sea; on frequent journeys, in danger from rivers, danger from robbers, danger from my own people, danger from Gentiles, danger in the city, danger in the wilderness, danger at sea, danger from false brothers; in toil and hardship, through many a sleepless night, in hunger and thirst, often without food, in cold and exposure. And, apart from other things, there is the daily pressure on me of my anxiety for all the churches (2 Corinthians 11:24–28).

But even Paul's many trials do not point to his faithful endurance as much as what he says about them: "For the sake of Christ, then, I am content with weaknesses, insults, hardships, persecutions, and calamities. For when I am weak, then I am strong" (2 Corinthians 12:10).

ENDURANCE MULTIPLIED

Females in Uzbekistan's majority-Muslim society are considered inferior to men. They lead hard lives of unending work around the home or farm. Christian women in Uzbekistan are doubly inferior and must run with an endurance brought about by faith in Christ.

An integral part of Uzbek culture in which women thrive, however, is hospitality. Women eagerly welcome visitors—especially during the long, cold winters—by taking a break and sharing tea. A team of Christian women in Uzbekistan is using this approach as a quiet means of church planting.

Olma came to faith two decades ago and immediately started several house churches with her husband. When authorities threatened to imprison them, they moved to another city, and when the police came after them again, they moved on to yet another city.

Everywhere Olma went, she taught new believers and led house fellowships. "I like when people come to Christ and their life changes," she said. "My biggest desire is revival in God's kingdom. My passion is to make more leaders; that way I can make disciples and send them back to their own communities."

And her faithful endurance continues to bear fruit. Umida, one of Olma's leaders in the disciple-making group, came to faith through the witness of an older sister, whom Oma had led to Christ. Umida's brothers had long treated her badly, telling her she was the ugliest girl they had ever seen. So when her older sister shared the Good News with her, Umida said, "It was easy for me to accept the gospel because in those days I needed peace and freedom."

Umida's sister visited her once a month, and they eagerly studied the Bible together. But when Umida's brothers learned about her new faith, they beat her, and her oldest brother took away her Bible and buried it. Umida remained faithful, however, and soon got a new Bible from Olma.

Over the next six years, Umida's brothers destroyed a total of six Bibles in an attempt to discourage their sister's newfound faith, breaking into the locked box in her room where she tried to keep God's Word safe. Despite her brothers' frequent beatings and ridicule, Umida maintained the faithful endurance that allowed her to keep growing in Christ.

Eventually, after discovering that her brothers were offering her to become the third wife of a seventy-eight-year-old man, Umida left home and moved in with Olma and her husband. They continued to disciple her for the next two years.

When Umida returned to her hometown, the Holy Spirit led her to follow her mentor's example. She started visiting a nearby village, drinking tea with other women and sharing the gospel. "For ten years, I didn't laugh at all," she said. "After coming to Christ, my heart was full of joy, and I wanted to share this joy with other people."

The testing of her faith not only built endurance in Umida's life, but it also has given her a heart of compassion for younger Christians in similar situations. "I know what persecution is," she explained, "and for this reason I like to pray for people who are in persecution, and I like to walk that path with them."

ENDURING UNTIL DEATH

Bounsaen is one of the oldest examples of faithful endurance we have today. But at age 101, he is still finding ways to minister in his country of Communist Laos and even hopes to attend Bible school. "My heart has just wanted to serve the Lord since I was twenty years old," he said. "Now I am tired physically, but my heart is not tired for the Lord's work."

When Bounsaen came to know Christ many years ago, he was working as a witch doctor, a common occupation among animistic tribes in Laos. "I was worshiping spirits," Bounsaen said. "I was a wicked and clueless person. When people talked about Jesus, I did not like it."

His attitude toward Christianity changed, however, when he fell in love with a Christian girl. "I saw her at first glance, and I wanted to marry her," Bounsaen said with a laugh. "She wanted to marry me too." His chosen spouse, a young woman named Term, lived in a village where a large number of people had come to faith in Christ during French colonization.

Determined to win Term's heart, Bounsaen went looking for a Bible. "I was reading the Bible all the time, and it made me know firmly that there is a God and he is real," he said. "I saw the truth deep down in my heart. That is why I wanted to passionately believe the Lord in my heart."

In retrospect, Bounsaen sees how God used his romantic attraction to bring him to Christ. Soon after coming to faith, Bounsaen led his parents and several others to the Lord. "Some of the village people who were worshiping spirits got sick, and the spirits did not cure them," he explained. "I went to pray for them, and they were healed. This opened many people's eyes."

Bounsaen continued to worship with Christians in his community during the country's civil war. Living in the only Christian village in the province, Christ-followers there welcomed the encouragement, fellowship, Bibles, and hymnals they received from believers in nearby Thailand—until the Communists won the war.

After the Lao Patriotic Front came to power in 1975, its members worked to eradicate Christianity from the newly acquired country, saving the harshest persecution for those who had been Christians for decades. "Many people renounced their faith during that time," recalled Bounsaen, who had by then become the leader of his church.

As the Communists' power increased throughout the 1970s, so did the pressure they placed on Christians. "Many came to persecute me," Bounsaen said. "They were police officers and some soldiers. They came to investigate and interrogate me three times."

He and fellow Christians endured other forms of persecution as well. While the Communists burned as many Bibles as they could find, villagers hid their copies of God's Word in the jungle.

"For my Bible, I wrapped it tightly with cloth and hid it in the trees," Bounsaen said. "When I wanted to read the Bible, I would go to the hiding spot and unwrap it. Those were some tough times. I and the other believers had to have so much patience."

Bounsaen was also forced to provide manual labor on building projects while receiving constant pressure to abandon his faith. He said authorities hoped to get rid of him so others would also renounce their faith. "They did not want others to be like me," he said. Ultimately, in December 1980, he was arrested and imprisoned for three months. But his faithful endurance carried him through.

"I was full of joy and happiness to the Lord in front of the police," he said. "I knew that the Lord would help me, because in the Bible the Lord said … 'Do not be afraid, as the Holy Spirit will be with you and prepare you for this.' I kept thinking like this and stood firm because of the Lord's words."

Released after completing a seminar on Communist principles in a forced effort to reindoctrinate him, Bounsaen was arrested two more times during the 1980s for his work as a pastor, serving a longer sentence each time. During that season of hardship, "They can do whatever they want," he told his congregation. "If they want to kill or keep us alive, it is up to them. We must be solid in this village. We cannot love our bodies. Our bodies will return to the land. Our spirit will be with the Lord. We have to stay solid in the Lord."

As the pressure from Communist authorities continued, so did the growth of Bounsaen's church. When authorities realized they weren't going to stop the Christians, the persecution waned at last—and the church grew even faster. Bounsaen said that now, "When we have our Christian celebrations, we invite the officials of the Lao Patriotic Front to come join us at the church."

Although he no longer preaches every week, Bounsaen sometimes gives the opening prayer for his church, and he continues to visit and pray for the sick. Although physically frail, his spirit remains strong. "I am really looking forward to the day that I am going to be with the Lord," he said. "All my sufferings in this world will be gone. . . . I am getting impatient, to be honest. He has prepared a home for me."

FOR REFLECTION AND DISCUSSION:

1. How can we recognize faithful endurance? What are some of the marks of a Christian who possesses this quality?
2. God granted endurance to Alban soon after he came to faith. Why do you think so many Christians take longer to show endurance in their lives?
3. The story of Moses, like many of our stories, is filled with spiritual highs and lows. Our lives, like Moses' life, are filled with spiritual highs as well as spiritual struggles. Think

about your life in the past few months or years. What spiritual highs have you experienced? Describe the circumstances. What spiritual lows have you experienced? How did the presence of God, who was evident and real to you in the times of thriving spiritually, give you the grace to endure the darkness of a spiritual valley?

4. Do you agree with Mr. Xi's statement that "We all know if we choose to work for the Lord, sometime, maybe not now, you will be persecuted for sure"? Why or why not?
5. Describe a time in your life—or in the life of a close friend or family member—when faithful endurance was displayed. What process, long or short, did God take them through as they developed it?

Visit vom.org/HeroicFaith to view Janette's story along with additional brief feature videos and digital resources.

HEROIC FAITH

CHAPTER 7

UNWAVERING OBEDIENCE

"Jesus loves us, and he invites us to be confident in that love. As we seek to obey him, we are not called to assess the risk involved and determine whether or not obedience will be beneficial or safe for us. We are simply called to trust and obey."

—Dan Baumann[1]

In 1668, Susanna Wesley was born into a world where the English government dictated the use of the Book of Common Prayer in all worship services. Christians were also forbidden from worshiping in groups larger than five people who were not their own family members unless a state official was present.

Soldiers destroyed houses where Christians met, took away books and furniture. Five thousand nonconformist Christians died in prison.

Although Susanna was associated at times with the official church, she refused to be a "Sunday-only" Christian. She was determined to obey God rather than the edicts of men when it came to living out her convictions. She began holding adult Christian education programs in her kitchen and conducted daily lessons with her children.

Her angry neighbors burned her fields and stabbed the three cows that provided milk to her family. They called her children "the little devils." One of her children, John Wesley, went on to become founder of the Methodists and led a great spiritual awakening in England.

Yet, despite the opposition, Susanna Wesley continued in her unwavering obedience to God.

CALLED TO OBEDIENCE

Susanna Wesley's heroic faith directed her actions—seek God first, and obey him, even in the face of opposition and harassment.

Aisha Granger has experienced those realities. The spiritual journey of this Nigerian woman, a member of the predominantly Muslim Fulani tribe, began with a desire to learn.

"I really wanted to go to school, but growing up in a Muslim environment as a Muslim girl, your orientation is toward growing up and being a good Muslim, a good mother," she explained. She followed the traditional path for female Muslims, marrying at age eighteen and giving birth to her first child a year later.

As Aisha continued to pursue being a good Muslim, she studied at the College of Islamic Studies in Bauchi and even became a state representative for the Federation of Muslim Women. She converted her living room into a mosque where women could pray, since Islam does not allow them to mix with men for prayer at the community mosque.

"I used to be a very fanatical Muslim," Aisha said. Her devotion to Islam continued until, in her twenties, she suffered from debilitating migraine headaches. None of the remedies offered by traditional healers helped her, including a last-ditch effort: reciting a Quranic passage four times before slaughtering four rams. If that did not work, the healers told her, she would die. When the ritual failed to alleviate her pain, she believed her death was imminent. Preparing to offer one final prayer, she went to the bathroom to perform her ceremonial washing.

But before she could complete this final task, she dropped to the floor, sensing a voice saying, "I want you to worship me." She had heard enough about Christianity to realize this voice had to be the God of the Bible, who interacts on a personal level.

This supernatural encounter sent Aisha on a four-year search for truth. She gradually stepped away from her leadership positions with Islamic women's groups and spent time alone in her living room, seeking God.

"I had never heard of salvation before in Islam," she said. "There's nothing like that. Your salvation is only by your good deeds. Even then, Allah will decide whether you go to paradise or not. There is no assurance."

As she studied the Bible and attended church, this young woman discovered the truth of the gospel: Jesus Christ had already accomplished on the cross everything necessary for her salvation. She simply needed to place her faith in him alone to gain freedom and eternal life. Soon, she was ready to tell her husband about her new faith.

Aisha's husband did not share her excitement; in fact, he sued her in Sharia (Islamic) court, demanding all her possessions and both of their children. If the case had remained there, the court would almost certainly have ruled against her. However, her doctor, pastor, and several others advocated for the case to be transferred to the magistrate court, and it was.

The magistrate gave her the choice of recanting her Christian faith or divorcing her husband. But since Aisha refused to give up her faith, her husband divorced her and gave her custody of the children.

But Aisha's struggles continued—and so did her obedience to Christ. In spite of her ex-husband relinquishing custody, her daughter refused to live with Aisha and remained with her father. And out of fear of violence from Muslims, other Christians didn't want to associate with Aisha. Even her own parents turned against her, accusing her of neglecting their needs by leaving her influential husband and his money. At one point, her ex-husband even burned down her house, causing her son to move back in with his father; the persecution was more than the child could bear.

A faithful God reached into her situation and rescued Aisha. Front-line workers helped her move to a new home in another neighborhood, where the community would not know she had left Islam. Before long, both her son and daughter not only accepted Christ but also came to live with her.

This brave mother eventually enrolled in seminary, determined to gain a firm theological foundation from which to teach others. And although Aisha lives with constant threats and the added stress of knowing her ex-husband and his family are still searching for her to kill her, she has no regrets. Her words reveal the heroic faith that fuels her daily choices to obey: "God created us to be his followers, to be worshiping him and being obedient to him."

COSTLY OBEDIENCE

Jesus encouraged his followers to "count the cost" before undertaking a ministry (Luke 14:28). But those with a more heroic faith do not base their obedience on its potential outcomes, whether positive or negative. Like Susanna Wesley and Aisha Granger, they follow Christ, so they obey him—no matter what.

Few people would understand this better than Dr. Hannelie Groenewald. She, her husband, Werner, and their two children left the relative safety of South Africa to serve in Afghanistan, convinced they were following God's purpose for their lives.

"We received this calling from the Lord that the Lord has got a purpose for us as a family to live out our love for him, our love for the Afghans, to serve," she said. "And here we are: God, take our lives and make with us whatever you find pleasing and good in your purpose."

But at times, the dangers of her adopted country led Hannelie to question God's call. As she explained, "I've asked myself many times in the past, 'Lord, is this where you really want us?' because of all the difficulties, the challenges. We can lose our lives any time for the Lord.

"When I look at that in the spiritual realm, I know that he will not take us to a place like Afghanistan and just dump us there [without having] a plan and a purpose for that," she added. "So I know 100% that we are in the right place, that we are obedient to the calling."

Hannelie's obedience led her to prepare her children for potential attacks because of their faith. "Jean-Pierre and Rodé, you will [someday] face a very difficult day, and I'm not going to be there to help you, and Daddy is also not going to be there to help you, but Jesus is going to help you through this, and he will be there," she told them. "He promised never to leave us nor forsake us."

And then it happened. Islamists stormed the office of the humanitarian aid group where the family worked and lived. In the end, Werner and both teenagers died, and their apartment was demolished when the Afghan military fired rocket-propelled grenades into the house.

Today, "I believe they are in front of the Lord's throne, worshiping, praising, glorifying him," Hannelie said. "And they are just waiting for me to finish the race as well."

Just as danger cannot stop a more heroic faith, threats of violence and even death cannot end the obedience it produces or the comfort

God brings: "God is our refuge and strength, a very present help in trouble. Therefore we will not fear though the earth give way, though the mountains be moved into the heart of the sea, though its waters roar and foam, though the mountains tremble at its swelling" (Psalm 46:1–3).

Hannelie's family gave everything to follow God in obedience. What are we willing to give?

OBEDIENT FATHER OF THE FAITH

As we have already seen, obeying God almost always includes personal sacrifice. God's calling of Abram (recorded in Genesis 12:1–3 and known as the Abrahamic Covenant) included one of the greatest promises recorded in history: "I will make of you a great nation, and I will bless you and make your name great, so that you will be a blessing. I will bless those who bless you, and him who dishonors you I will curse, and in you all the families of the earth shall be blessed" (vv. 2–3). But the calling and the promise to the one who would later be known as Abraham and the "father of the faith" came at great personal cost.

His obedience, which carried that cost, earned him a prominent place in Hebrews 11. In fact, the author of Hebrews devotes more verses in that chapter to the faith of Abraham than to that of any other biblical figure.

One descriptive phrase in Genesis describes what was both obedience and a test of Abraham's faith: "Abram went, as the LORD had told him" (Genesis 12:4). Despite the cost of leaving family, friends, and the familiar setting; despite his age (seventy-five); despite the distance (more than four hundred miles), he followed God in wholehearted obedience.

In Stephen's sermon before the council of Jewish elders (Acts 7:2–53), he says God first called Abraham to Haran when he lived in Mesopotamia. It was only after Abraham's father, Terah, died that God extended the call to the land of Canaan. And when he did, as the Bible says, Abraham—along with his wife, Sarai, and nephew Lot—went, taking with them all their belongings.

The journey was not perfect, and neither was Abraham. We may think first of his failures—persuading Sarai to lie on his behalf (Genesis 12:11–13) and, later, accepting her misguided plan to help God fulfill his promise that her husband would become the father of many nations. Abraham's failure to trust God's plan was evident when he took it upon himself to bear a child with her maid, Hagar.

But rather than highlighting Abraham's sin, God instead uses the writer of Hebrews to honor his faith. He "went out, not knowing where he was going" and "by faith he went to live in the land of promise" (Hebrews 11:8–9).

Here, the writer of Hebrews brings in another element that reveals the extent of Abraham's faith. When he reached the promised land, he chose a temporary rather than a permanent dwelling, living in tents as a traveler or sojourner would.

When we read this story, we tend to focus on the promised land and its riches of overflowing milk and honey. But the depth of Abraham's faith—which brought about his obedience—moved his focus from the benefits of a lavish promised land to the giver of the promise. The land itself was not the final fulfillment but an earthly picture of the eternal promise: heaven itself and life forever with God (v. 10).

The verses about the promised land, however, are not the only ones in Hebrews 11 that refer to Abraham. In verses 17–19, we read of his "offering up" his only son, another picture of the not-yet-realized gift of God in his only Son, Jesus Christ.

The full story of the sacrifice, given in Genesis 22:1–19, reveals the growth of Abraham's obedience to God. When God told him to give up his long-awaited son, he did not make excuses. He did not hesitate. He did not argue.

In response to God's test, "Abraham rose early in the morning, saddled his donkey, and took two of his young men with him, and his son Isaac. And he cut the wood for the burnt offering and arose and went to the place of which God had told him" (Genesis 22:3). Those actions did not come from a reluctant or rebellious heart but from one that trusted God with everything he had—including his treasured son.

What we love easily becomes our idol. In Abraham's case, his willingness to obey God's command shows his deep trust of a loving Father. The same God who had moved him from Mesopotamia to Haran and on to the promised land, the same God who had sustained him through drought, dissension, and desperation, would surely deliver Isaac from death. And, as we read in Genesis 22:13, he did just that, providing a ram from a nearby thicket just as Abraham was poised, knife raised high, to sacrifice his son.

God's faithfulness brought Abraham to the promised land, and God's faithfulness provided the sacrificial ram. But Abraham's obedience set the stage to showcase that faithfulness. And Abraham's obedience to God also made him an example of the more heroic faith that we continue to emulate today.

DELAYED OBEDIENCE

Have you ever known that God wanted you to do something, yet you refused? Most of us have likely had this experience, and so did

Aqil, who leads an evangelical church in Jordan. The country, like much of the Middle East, is almost 100% Muslim. Threats and pressure against Christians' work—especially any kind of outreach to Muslims—are not uncommon.

After the civil war heated up in neighboring Syria, destroying that nation from the inside, tens of thousands of refugees streamed into Jordan. Aqil was aware of the refugees' arrival and vaguely aware of their terrible struggle to eke out a life in his country. But as the pastor of a church, he already had a ministry. He had already faced pressure.

That's why, when a donor called the church and offered funding to help Aqil give aid to Syrian refugees, he politely answered, "No, thank you." His task list was full. He wasn't looking for new avenues of service or additional ways to fill up his weekly calendar.

But God didn't seem concerned about Aqil's busy schedule. And Aqil clearly sensed the Lord telling him not to close his heart to either the refugees or the ministry opportunity.

After a night of not sleeping well, arguing with God, Aqil knew what he must do. He spoke with the donor again and told him yes, he would be willing to deliver aid if the offer was still available.

And so a ministry began. Aqil and others from his church began traveling to an area where thousands of refugees lived in makeshift shelters, tents, or whatever they could find. They had no way of supporting themselves, and their children were not welcome in local schools.

The refugees came from many different faith streams, all desperate, all far from home. In addition to giving humanitarian aid, Aqil and the team from his church offered prayer. Every time, they made it clear they would be praying to Jesus Christ—*Isa al Masih*—not to Allah or Muhammad. It was rare that anyone turned down their offer of prayer. The refugees were, after all, desperate for help; what could asking Jesus hurt?

One day, the Christians were in the home of a woman and her children, and again the pastor offered to pray. The woman agreed, mentioning that her son had struggled with a heart defect since birth. Aqil and his team prayed over this family in the name of Isa al Masih before leaving to deliver aid to others. At the end of the day, they returned to their city.

A few days later, Aqil's phone rang. The woman whose son had a heart defect was calling.

"I need you to write down the prayer that you prayed for my son," she said.

This confused the pastor. "Okay, I guess I can write it down. But can you tell me why you need to have the prayer written down?"

"It's the heart murmur that my son had, the one he's had since birth. The heart murmur is gone now! The doctors say there's no sign that he's ever had any heart issues at all! I need you to write down the prayer you prayed because I want to say that prayer over my other children as well."

Muslims are told exactly what to pray to Allah and how to pray it. Since this woman had seen Jesus heal her son, she wanted to pray to him now. But she wanted to make sure she had the correct words to say.

Smiling with delight, Aqil praised the Lord for healing the boy. He also explained to the mother that it wasn't special words that led to her son's healing but rather that the prayers were directed to Jesus Christ, the Son of God. He had heard their prayers, answered them, and brought healing to the little boy's heart.

It didn't take long for that mother to decide she wanted to follow Isa al Masih, the One who hears and answers our prayers. And it didn't take long for Aqil to see how God was working. Even though Aqil had delayed at first, God still honored his obedience. God had allowed Christians to offer help in places where Muslims would not. God had miraculously provided for needs, healed the sick, and had even moved Muslims, including some Islamic leaders, to leave Islam and follow Jesus. These stories were not once-a-year wonders; they became weekly, almost expected, occurrences.

The time Aqil spent working with refugees became his favorite time of the week; the place he felt the most fulfilled in his work. It was the place God seemed to move most clearly and often. Following God in obedience—in the ministry he had first tried to avoid—brought Aqil absolute excitement and lasting joy.[2]

BROKEN, YET OBEDIENT

Dan Baumann's voice still trembles when he speaks of his nine weeks in an Iranian prison in 1997. But his heroic faith is evident and carried him through imprisonment and beatings to a place of deep trust and wholehearted obedience to God.

Dan traveled to Afghanistan, where he worked in a hospital for ten years, and during that time, he fell in love with Muslims. "It changed my life," he said of his time living and working there.

Following God's direction, Dan and a friend planned a two-week trip to Iran over Christmas break. As an American, Dan couldn't enter Iran using his U.S. passport. But because Dan's dad was a Swiss citizen, Dan was a dual citizen and was able to use his Swiss passport.

But at the end of their two-week trip, their plans changed. When Dan and his friend reached a border checkpoint, officials told them something was wrong with their passports. They were instructed to travel fifteen hours to a location in the Iranian city of Tehran where they could resolve the issue.

When Dan and his friend arrived at the location, officials initially treated them kindly and led them to separate rooms. But it was in those rooms that the beatings began.

"For about six hours, they kicked me and spat on me and hit me; there was no clear explanation, other than to accuse me of lying about my citizenship," Dan said. "I felt these words come to my heart, 'You are going to be here for nine weeks.'"

From the beginning of his incarceration, Dan was assured of God's presence with him. He would need that assurance, as he was beaten every day by the same man, with no explanation.

While Dan longed for earthly justice, God wanted to teach him something eternal. "Dan, I want to teach you to love your enemies," Dan sensed the Lord saying. "Ask me what I think about the man who is beating you."

Dan wrestled with the question but finally relented and asked God what he thought of his persecutor. As Dan was beaten, he began to see his torturer through God's eyes and realized God loved him. And as Dan became overwhelmed by God's love for this man, God began to change Dan's heart.

Within two weeks, Dan heard rumors that he would be in prison for a minimum of nine months and other rumors of a multi-year imprisonment. Shortly after hearing this news, depression set in, and with it, the temptation to take his life.

After four failed attempts to commit suicide, he fell to the ground, aware of his brokenness, shame, and desperation.

God met Dan in this brokenness with a vision of Jesus standing in front of him—not an angry Jesus, but one whose face was filled with kindness, love, and acceptance. "As I stared into this very caring, kind face, I saw these hands come underneath me, and God speak these loving words: 'Dan, I love you, and if you will let me, I will carry you through this time.'

"From that day until today, I've never had those [suicidal] thoughts again," Dan said. "In the midst of my brokenness, God met me. God was still good, and he met me and gave me hope."

After five weeks, Dan's friend was released. Soon, Dan faced another test of his obedience as guards loaded him into a van. "You're going to a courthouse," they told him.

As he walked into a courtroom filled with people and video cameras, Dan stood on the witness stand in his prison clothes, trembling. The judge walked in, looked straight at Dan, knowing he had been given two death sentences, and said, "Tell us today, why—why did you come to Iran?"

As Dan continued shaking in fear, he recalled what Matthew 10:19 said about not being afraid when called before authorities: "What you are to say will be given to you in that hour."

Looking at the judge, Dan told him the truth: "I came here to tell you about Jesus Christ."[3]

Dan did not receive punishment for his witness, but officials did not release him from prison. That did not happen until nine long weeks had passed—the exact amount of time he sensed the Lord telling him when he was first arrested.

"Ultimately, we have nothing to fear. Jesus loves us, and he invites us to be confident in that love," Dan said. Counting the cost of our obedience is a moment-by-moment practice for biblical disciples who, knowing the price they will pay, trust God as they walk in obedience.

DECLARATION OF FAITHFUL DISOBEDIENCE

Pastor Wang Yi's faith also cost him his earthly freedom—albeit for a much longer time than Dan Baumann. Yet this pastor, who is Christ's witness in Chengdu, China, continues to obey God at any cost.

A well-known lawyer, writer, and law professor, Wang Yi founded a Bible study in his home in 2004. He later resigned his position at Chengdu University to follow his Christian calling. The Bible study became Early Rain Covenant Church, an independent, or unregistered (illegal), church in 2008. Later named the church's lead pastor, Wang Yi became a prominent member of the house church movement.

Despite the church's illegal status, Early Rain, which grew quickly, didn't conceal its worship and missional position. The church's strategy: to hide nothing from the government and to hold fast to its Christian convictions.

"The Bible teaches us that in all matters relating to the gospel and human conscience, we must obey God and not men," Wang Yi wrote. "For this reason, spiritual disobedience and bodily suffering are both ways we testify to another, eternal world and to another, glorious King."

Wang Yi's boldness—and the stands Early Rain took against abortion and other areas of injustice it saw in the Chinese Communist Party—ultimately led to his arrest in December 2018, along with his wife, Jiang Rong, and more than 100 other church members. Although most were released quickly, Wang Yi remained in prison, facing trial the following December. No verdict was announced, but authorities later found Wang Yi guilty of subverting the Chinese Communist Party. Because Wang Yi led his church to obey God rather than man, the Communist rulers viewed his influence as a threat to their plan. They intended to bring everything within China under the influence of the Chinese Communist Party, which includes limiting Christian families in discipling their own children.

Wang Yi is serving a nine-year prison sentence. But despite ongoing persecution, Early Rain church members continue to stand for Christ. Days after his arrest, the church published Wang Yi's "Declaration of Faithful Disobedience," which he had left with instructions to publish if he were detained for more than forty-eight hours.

"I firmly believe that Christ has called me to carry out this faithful disobedience through a life of service, under this regime that opposes the gospel and persecutes the church," he wrote. "The goal of disobedience is not to change the world, but to testify about another world."

"Faithful disobedience," as Wang Yi puts it, is a necessary expression of unwavering obedience to God.

Wang Yi's life and testimony reveal the depth of his faith and the extent of his obedience, both standing as powerful examples for us all.

FOR REFLECTION AND DISCUSSION:

1. What do you think of when you hear the word "obedience"? How is (or is not) obedience to God different from what comes to your mind?
2. How would you describe Susanna Wesley's faith? What demonstrates to a watching world that your faith is beyond that of a "Sunday-only" Christian?
3. How did God prepare Hannelie and her family for the ultimate death of Werner and their two children?
4. Have you ever delayed, or been tempted to delay, your obedience to God as Aqil did? If so, why? What happened when you did?

5. While in prison, Dan Baumann struggled with his own brokenness. How did a wholehearted obedience set him free even before he was released?

Visit vom.org/HeroicFaith to view Hannelie's story along with additional brief feature videos and digital resources.

CHAPTER 8

STEADFAST LOVE

"In solitary confinement, we could not pray as before . . . We were as weak as skeletons. The Lord's Prayer was much too long for us—we could not concentrate enough to say it. My only prayer repeated again and again was, 'Jesus, I love You.'"

—Richard Wurmbrand

Do you know what lovesickness is—to love someone to madness? This is love that instead of drawing on its own large resources demands even more love. It is better to have this dissatisfied love for Jesus, than a satisfied love for the world.

Valya was a twelve-year-old girl in Communist Russia. One day the director of her school decided she should become a member of the Communist children's movement known as the Young Pioneers. She refused. Her refusal was invalid since the director had legal rights over her, just like parents have in the free world.

Enrollment day arrived. The chosen candidates stood before a table where three-pointed Pioneer scarves lay. One by one the girls stepped forward to don the scarf and take the oath.

"Valya Vastchenko," called the director. "Valya, step forward. Take the oath."

Valya's mouth stayed tightly shut.

"Say the oath, Valya! Very well. I will read it in your name." The director pointed to two other girls. "Place the scarf around her neck as I read." He began. "I, Valya, pioneer of the USSR, promise before my comrade-patriots who decide the question of my admission to the organization, that I will stand firmly for the cause of Lenin and the victory of communism. I promise …"

His next words were drowned out as Valya burst into prayer to God and began to sing a hymn: "We will stand firm for the faith, for Christ, following His example."

That child knew from the experience of many others that she had destroyed her career possibilities for the rest of her life. She knew she might be put into an atheistic boarding school. She knew her parents might be put in prison and might even die there, but she did not rationalize. She loved Jesus to madness, so she could not do other than what she did.

When Thomas Aquinas died, he was discussing the Song of Solomon. He wrote a song titled, "I adore You," expressing his love and desire for Jesus:

> Jesus, whom for the present, veiled I see,
> What I so long for, Oh! Vouch safe to me,
> That I may see Your beauteous face unfolding.
> And maybe blessed, Your glory in beholding.[1]

The bride is lovesick. Therefore, she suffers. Biblical disciples are lovesick. Our steadfast love of God demonstrates a heroic faith to a world that might declare it madness, yet we willingly choose love.

"AFTER GOD'S OWN HEART"

As we return to Hebrews 11, we see many of those with a heroic faith exhibit the same love as Valya: love for God when others might view it as madness. Perhaps none of these individuals is more flawed than David. However, none demonstrated God's love in a more consistent manner than the shepherd boy turned psalmist, king, and defender of Israel. David had the kind of deep faith that yields a steadfast love.

Although he receives a mere mention in Hebrews 11 as part of a long list of biblical figures, David makes frequent appearances in Scripture. Sixty-six Old Testament chapters are devoted to him, along with nearly the same number in the New Testament.

David's love for God was forged through the power of trials—and also a humility that led him to seek and offer forgiveness. Rather than being sent to the battlefield, this youngest of eight sons was relegated to the flocks and fields, where he poured out his love for God in words and music. After he became known for soothing King Saul's often-angry spirit by playing his lyre—and was later appointed as the king's armor-bearer (1 Samuel 17)—his faith-filled victory over Goliath moved him into a position as leader over Saul's armies (1 Samuel 18:5).

But it didn't take long for jealousy to twist its way into Saul's relationship with David. When women danced before Saul and David after their victory over the Philistines, saying, "Saul has struck down his thousands, and David his ten thousands" (1 Samuel 18:7), Saul hurled his spear twice at David in attempts to take the younger man's life. Scripture says, "Saul was afraid of David because the LORD was with him but had departed from Saul" (1 Samuel 18:12; read the whole story in 1 Samuel 18:6–16).

Saul's attacks continued—so much so that David became a fugitive, running to protect his life (1 Samuel 21–23). First Samuel 24 contains the powerful story of a choice David made in the wilderness of Engedi. Hidden in a cave where an unsuspecting Saul entered, David could easily have taken the king's life. Instead, he made the choice to forgive and honor him as "the Lord's anointed" (vv. 6, 10)—a choice based not on what Saul deserved but on David's love and respect for his heavenly Father as well as for a fallible, yet God-anointed king.

Through these trials, David's love for God grew. He began Psalm 18, in which he praised God for deliverance from Saul, with a declaration of love: "I love you, O Lord my strength" (Psalm 18:1). Psalm 63 also reflects David's deep love for God—even during the disastrous circumstance of fleeing from his son Absalom, the leader of a revolt against his father's reign:

"O God, you are my God; earnestly I seek you; my soul thirsts for you; my flesh faints for you, as in a dry and weary land where there is no water. So I have looked upon you in the sanctuary, beholding your power and glory. Because your steadfast love is better than life, my lips will praise you. So I will bless you as long as I live; in your name I will lift up my hands" (vv.1–4).

However, when we think of the biblical stories of David, we remember more than his deep faith and steadfast love for God. We remember more than his great prowess as a warrior, the forgiveness he extended to King Saul, and his own mighty anointing as king. We remember his illicit liaison with Bathsheba and his wicked order of the murder of her husband, Uriah (see 2 Samuel 11).

But if we remember the depth of his sin, we must also remember his immediate and fervent repentance when the prophet Nathan called him to account. Rather than offering excuses, responding in anger, or attempting to deflect, David made a simple statement: "I have sinned against the Lord" (2 Samuel 12:13).

The heartbreak David demonstrated over his sin—and the gut-wrenching confession recorded in Psalm 51—could have come only from one with the kind of heroic faith that moved him to love God with all his heart. No wonder the prophet Samuel, in referring to David, described him as "a man after [God's] heart" (1 Samuel 13:14; see also Acts 13:22). Forged in faith and transformed by trials, David's heart reflected God's heart of love.

LOVE IS STRONGER THAN DEATH

As the work bus trundled along, Alex wasn't thinking about God or his love. Exhausted from studying late the night before, he turned his thoughts to the long hours he would spend in the banana fields with his fellow day laborers.

Suddenly, guerrillas belonging to the FARC (Revolutionary Armed Forces of Colombia) ordered the bus carrying Alex and the other farm workers to stop. Climbing aboard, one of the militants demanded the driver tell him where the bus was going; others brandished their guns at the terrified passengers.

"The guerrillas told us that they would not hurt anybody, that there wasn't anything to worry about, but we knew they were lying," Alex said. Herded into the back of the bus, he and the others watched as the guerrillas forced the driver to keep going.

"We didn't know where they were taking us or what they would do to us," Alex said. "We drove for, like, another twenty minutes, and then they made everyone get out."

Screaming and crying, the passengers became even more fearful as the guerrillas made them kneel beside the road. Alex was in the first row.

"Many were crying or begging, but God gave me courage," he said. "I tried to stop my friend from pleading with the guerrillas. I told him that only God has control of his life—he should be speaking with God, but he just kept pleading for his life."

The pleading did Alex's friend no good. In an instant, an angry guerrilla fired a bullet, killing the man instantly.

"At that moment, I believed I was going to die," Alex said. And in that moment, his heroic faith moved him toward an expression of steadfast love for God. Boldly, he sang his praise: "*Tu felididad es grande, tu felididad, incomparable*" ("Your faithfulness is great; your faithfulness, incomparable"). Angered, a guerrilla struck him, and Alex fell to the ground.

The guerrillas continued firing their guns, mowing down the kneeling passengers, then walking among them to see if any remained alive.

"My country has suffered from much violence," Alex said. "My father was killed by the guerrillas when I was only sixteen. And now, I would join him in heaven. I was ready to die, if even by the hands of terrorists. But then I had one regret: I had not told them about Jesus."

All the other passengers lost their lives that day, but Alex's story did not end on the side of the road. His testimony reveals both his faith and the love for God and for others that came as its fruit.

"I heard them yell to make sure everyone was dead," Alex said. "I had been shot in the leg and face, and was surprised to still be alive. And still, I wanted to tell them about Jesus."

Years after his recovery, while ministering inside a prison, Alex met the guerrilla who had tried to kill him. That imprisoned guerrilla commander is now a follower of Christ, and Alex is his teacher, continuing to demonstrate the steadfast love produced by his heroic faith.

COUNTING THE SCARS

"One, two, three, ..." began Temistocres Ngabona, as he counted the scars on his leg. "Four, five, six, seven, eight ...," he continued, moving to his right arm and then to his severed thumb and mangled fingers. When he reached the ninth scar, he buried his face in his arms, overcome with emotion, while recalling the attack that nearly ended his life.

Temistocres' steadfast love of Christ was birthed when he and his wife, Deborah, heard the gospel and became devoted Christians in northern Tanzania, a predominantly Muslim area. As he grew in his faith, Temistocres and some fellow church members committed to praying every night. They met at the church at 9:00 or 10:00 p.m., after which a few people remained and took turns sleeping and praying throughout the night.

A mosque was located less than a mile away from the church, and the local Muslim community took notice of the Christians' prayer meetings. Though believers can practice their faith openly in majority-Christian Tanzania, Temistocres' town is near the Ugandan border, and radical Muslims in the area occasionally exerted their influence. Attacks on homes and churches were possible, and intense pressure from family members was not uncommon.

One day during a meeting at the mosque, a swarm of bees filled the building and disrupted the service. Some of the Muslims blamed the praying Christians for the insect invasion, believing the

Christ-followers had cursed the mosque. Their anger toward the nightly prayer group rose to a point of violence.

Temistocres fell asleep one night as he and a friend were praying at the church. He was startled awake as a man wearing a headlamp swung a large machete at his head. A group of men from the mosque had come to attack anyone at the church.

Temistocres' left leg was nearly severed just above his ankle. Another man struck him with a large knife three more times before the attackers ran off. Sadly, Temistocres' friend didn't survive. The attackers had struck him in the head, and he died.

Slowly pulling himself, half crawling and half sliding, out the church door, across the ground, through a field, and onto a path, Temistocres prayed someone might find him. About 2:30 a.m., a woman discovered him and brought him some water. She also called the authorities, who eventually took him to the hospital.

Temistocres' steadfast love for Christ, which was grounded in the forgiveness he received from the Lord, gave him the ability to forgive his attackers. The man arrested for the assault and murder was released for unknown reasons, and Temistocres has even seen his attackers in the city. He still chooses to show them grace. "They are forgiven," he said. "I know that they did something that they didn't know, like Jesus said, 'Father, forgive them, for they know not what they do.'"

While Temistocres' scars bear evidence of the brutal attack and are a reminder of the death of his friend, he continues to serve Christ faithfully.

Those with a more heroic faith pursue Christ with a steadfast love—a love that takes seriously Paul's words: "For it has been granted to you that for the sake of Christ you should not only believe in him but also suffer for his sake" (Philippians 1:29).

"TWO THINGS I CAN'T LIVE WITHOUT"

Yona Kanamuzeyi is another who demonstrated a heroic faith by his steadfast love for God and his willingness to serve him at any cost. Yona was born to a mixed marriage of enemy tribes—Hutu and Tutsi—in Rwanda. Raised in the Christian faith, he accepted a difficult assignment. God called him to serve his fellow Rwandans, who were left homeless by the tribal violence and then resettled in the 1960s by the government. Eventually, Yona became a pastor in the Nyamata district, responsible for twenty-four churches with about six thousand total members.

In addition to pastoring, Yona helped distribute relief supplies to the displaced. He first met with Christian refugees in the shade of a large tree, reading passages from the Bible that reminded them the Lord was their shelter and shade.

He initially moved to the area by himself. After he got a house, his wife, Mary, and their children joined him. Those around him marveled at the couple's love for each other.

"Doesn't he ever beat or curse you?" women would ask Mary.

"No, he doesn't," she responded. "Sometimes he asks my forgiveness, and I his. And Jesus forgives us. And we pray together." Such a love was rare in Rwanda.

In this era, Tutsis who fled into surrounding countries used terrorist tactics to fight back against Hutu control in Rwanda. The terrorists were called *inyenzi,* or cockroaches. As people's fear grew, they suspected any Tutsi of being a terrorist. After the inyenzi tried twice to invade Rwanda, anyone with suspected inyenzi connections was arrested by the army. Some were executed. Some were thrown into prison, where many died from the overcrowding and lack of medical care.

Despite the turmoil, Yona continued his ministry work, welcoming Christians to his home—in spite of a curfew—for late-night prayer meetings.

In January 1964, a friend warned Yona that he was going to be killed. When Yona asked why, the friend said it was because of his belief in the Word of God and the way he loved everyone.

"The Word of God and the love of God are two things I can't live without," Yona replied.

He told Mary about the threat, and the couple prayed together. "God, you called me and sent me here," Yona prayed. "You know me, the days I've already lived, and the days which remain. If it's your will to call me home, I'm ready."

On the evening of January 23, five Rwandan soldiers arrived at the family residence in an open jeep, demanding Yona come with them for questioning. The family knew when soldiers came for someone at night, that person was never seen again. Two others from the village were also apprehended.

The soldiers drove north until they reached the bridge over the Nyaborongo River, where they ordered the prisoners out of the jeep and forced them to put all their possessions in a pile. Before he laid down his journal, Yona wrote inside it, "We are going to heaven." He spoke with the two other prisoners about their salvation, and together they sang, "There is a happy land . . . where saints in glory stand."

Yona asked the sergeant to return his diary and money to his wife. "You had better pray to your God," the soldier replied.

Yona did, with the following words: "Lord God, you know that we have not sinned against the government, and now I pray you, in your mercy, accept our lives. And we pray you to avenge our innocent blood and help these soldiers who do not know what they are doing."

Yona was tied up and marched out onto the bridge, singing as he went: "There's a land that is fairer than day. And by faith, we can see it afar. Where the Father waits over the way. To prepare us a dwelling place there."

The soldier ended the song with a gunshot. Yona's body was dumped in the river.

His friend, Andrew Kayumba, also tied and ready to be shot, was instead driven home with a stern warning to never speak about Pastor Kanamuzeyi's execution. Andrew escaped from Rwanda and told what he had seen, and about the courage of his friend, whose steadfast love for God moved him to pray for his executioner and walk, singing, to his death.

SURPRISED BY LOVE

What do you do when you face the person who murdered your entire family? What do you do when that person is now a brother in Christ?

Sabina Wurmbrand faced that exact situation. When Romania first entered World War II, tens of thousands of Jews had already been killed or deported. Because Richard and Sabina lived in Bucharest in 1939, their lives were spared. But Sabina's Jewish parents, three sisters, young brother, and other relatives who lived in Bukovina were rounded up and sent to Transnistria, a desolate border province annexed from Russia.

The treacherous journey to Transnistria claimed the lives of many; starvation, humiliation, and brutal execution awaited those who arrived. There, in a sweeping genocide, every member of Sabina's family was murdered.

When Richard told her of the savage killings, Sabina crumbled, sobbing. *I will never see my mother and father again*, she thought. *I will never again embrace my sisters or my brother. How did they die? Who took their lives?*

But that was the last time Richard ever saw his wife weep for her family. "I'm not going to cry," she said, straightening her shoulders and slowing her breath. "You should have a happy wife . . . our church deserves a servant with courage."

Not long afterward, the Wurmbrands' landlord, a devout Christian, told Richard about a soldier staying in his home. "I knew him before the war, but he's changed completely," the landlord said, wringing his hands. "He's become an absolute brute who boasts about how he volunteered to exterminate Jews in Transnistria. He brags about killing hundreds with his own hands."

Transnistria? Richard felt a chill run down his spine. *Can it be?*

During dinner with Sabina and their son, Richard kept the news to himself, turning it over in his mind. That night, his thoughts raced, and God would not let him sleep. He crawled out of bed and went upstairs to the landlord's apartment to have an all-night prayer vigil. He knocked on the door, and when it opened, he saw the silhouette of a soldier, lounging in the living room.

As the landlord made introductions, the soldier stood to his feet, towering over Richard. His name was Borila, a battle-seasoned veteran who bragged about slaughtering countless Jews.

As he listened to the stories, Richard's feelings wavered between rage and sorrow. When Borila paused, Richard interjected. "It's a frightening story, but I'm not scared for the Jews. God will compensate them for what they've suffered."

He looked squarely at the soldier. "I'm anguished thinking about what will happen to their murderers when they stand before God's judgment seat."

Borila leaped from his chair, a large vein pulsing in his thick neck. The landlord jumped up as well, fearing what might come next. Borila and Richard were guests in his home, and he couldn't allow a brawl. Borila eyed Richard suspiciously but then regained composure and returned to his lounge chair.

Over the course of the evening, the conversation drifted to more neutral topics. Borila, a music enthusiast, described how, while stationed in Ukraine, he'd fallen in love with the local songs.

Richard saw an opportunity. *The fish has entered my net!* he thought. "If you'd like to hear some of them, come down to my flat," he told Borila. "I'm definitely no pianist, but I can play a few Ukrainian melodies."

While his family slept, Richard welcomed the two men to his flat and softly played the songs Borila loved. The soldier's eyes welled up, and his face turned red. Like David, the Jewish shepherd boy who played the harp before King Saul, Richard knew the music was having a profound effect.

It didn't take long for Richard to exhaust his repertoire. Sliding his hands from the piano keys, he turned and faced the murderer. "I have something very important to tell you."

Borila wiped his eyes. "Go on."

"If you were to look through that curtain, you'd see that someone's asleep in the next room," Richard said, gesturing toward the wall. "It's my wife, Sabina. Her parents, her sisters, and her twelve-year-old brother were killed with the rest of her family." The soldier glanced at the curtained room. "You told me that you killed hundreds of Jews near Golta."

Borila nodded.

"That's where they were taken. You yourself don't know whom you've shot, so we can assume you're the man who murdered her family."

Borila jumped up from his chair, but Richard held up his hand. "Wait. I want to try something. Let's do an experiment. I'm going to wake up my wife and tell her who you are and what you've done. And I can tell you exactly what will happen."

Borila looked at the pastor, bewildered.

"My wife won't speak one word of reproach to you," Richard assured him. "In fact, she'll hug you like you're her brother, and she'll bring you the best supper she can find in this house."

Borila couldn't believe his ears. After all, he had murdered her family—wouldn't she demand his blood?

But Richard continued, "So if Sabina, who's a sinner like all of us, can forgive and love like this, imagine how Jesus, who is perfect love, can love and forgive you. If you turn to him, everything you've done will be forgiven."

Borila's hard exterior crumbled. Guilt and forgiveness colliding in his heart, he clutched his shirt and ripped it apart. "Oh God, what do I do? What do I do?" he sobbed, cradling his head in his hands. "I'm a murderer. I'm soaked in blood. *What do I do?*"

"In the name of the Lord Jesus Christ, I command the devil of hatred to leave your soul!" Richard declared.

Borila trembled as the two men prayed aloud together. Over and over, the killer asked God to forgive him. When Borila had exhausted himself, Richard told him, "I promised you an experiment, and I'm going to keep my word."

He drew back the curtain and slipped into Sabina's room. "There's a man here you have to meet," he whispered, patting her shoulder. She rubbed her eyes and sat up. "I believe he's the man who murdered your family, but he's repented, and now he's our brother."

Sabina wrapped herself in a robe, sat in silence for a few minutes, and then went to greet her family's murderer. She surprised him with an embrace, and the two held each other and wept, kissing each other's cheeks again and again.

Richard knew his wife's heart. If God could forgive her for the sins in her own past, she could forgive Borila. Richard also knew God's love was stronger than the atrocities Borila had committed, strong enough to fill his wife's heart with the love she needed to forgive the brutal soldier.

Soon the time came for Borila to rejoin his regiment in a neighboring town. His unit had been ordered back to the front lines, and he had to make a decision.

"What do I do?" he asked Richard. "I'll have to start killing again."

"No, you've killed more than a soldier needs to," Richard said, wrapping his arms around his newfound brother. "Better allow others to kill you instead. The Bible doesn't forbid that."

Borila nodded, put on his military cap, and departed. Over time he became one of the Wurmbrands' closest friends. The only two men Sabina ever kissed after her marriage were her husband and the man who murdered her family. Her heroic faith had brought about a love that conquered unforgiveness and hatred, turning bitter to sweet and bringing enduring beauty from the enemy's ashes.

FOR REFLECTION AND DISCUSSION:

1. What does it mean to love someone or something? What sets the love described in this chapter apart from other kinds of loves?

2. What would have to be true for your own spiritual devotion to be described as "lovesick" with God?
3. Do you think David's life demonstrates steadfast love? Why or why not?
4. How would you share the gospel with someone who had attempted to kill you? If possible, role-play the situation Alex faced when he met his would-be murderer in prison and practice telling the good news of Christ.
5. Do you think you could have remained faithful to Christ, as Temistocres did following his life-threatening attack? Why or why not? How did his love for Christ propel him to continue to serve faithfully?
6. More than one story in this chapter shows the power of God's love in forgiveness. Describe a time when you forgave someone who had deeply hurt you. How did your faith and love influence your actions?

Visit vom.org/HeroicFaith to view Alex's story along with additional brief feature videos and digital resources.

END NOTES

CHAPTER 1

[1] Elisabeth Elliot, *Through Gates of Splendor,* 50th ed. (Carol Stream, Illinois: Tyndale Momentum, 1981), 249.

[2] Elisabeth Elliot, *The Savage My Kinsman* (New York: Harper & Brothers, 1961), 157.

[3] Ellen Vaughn, *Becoming Elisabeth Elliot* (Nashville: B&H Publishing Group, 2020), 207.

[4] Elliot, *Through Gates of Splendor,* 249.

[5] Todd Nettleton, *When Faith Is Forbidden* (Chicago, Moody Publishers, 2021), 62–63.

[6] Nettleton, *When Faith,* 63.

[7] Nettleton, 64.

[8] Nettleton, 65.

[9] Nettleton, 65.

[10] Nettleton, 65.

[11] Letter from Betty Elliot to missionary supporters, Oct. 4, 1958, https://elisabethelliot.org/about/timeline/; Item 39 of 84.

CHAPTER 2

[1] Brother Lawrence, *The Practice of the Presence of God: The Best Rule of Holy Life* (London: The Epworth Press, n.d.), "Fourth Conversation."

[2] Brother Lawrence, *Practice,* "Fifth Letter."

[3] Brother Lawrence, *Practice,* "Fourth Conversation."

[4] Brother Lawrence, *Practice,* "Fourth Conversation."

CHAPTER 3

[1] Charles Haddon Spurgeon, "Joseph's Bones," Dec. 18, 1870, in *Metropolitan Tabernacle Pulpit*, Vol. 16, https://www.spurgeon.org/resource-library/sermons/josephs-bones/#flipbook/, accessed Oct. 31, 2022.

CHAPTER 4

[1] E.H. Hamilton, *Afraid? Of What? And Other Poems and Sketches* (Hong Kong: Cathay Press, 1960), 4–7.

CHAPTER 6

[1] Nettleton, *When Faith,* 143–144.

[2] Nettleton, *When Faith*, 141–144.

CHAPTER 7

[1] Dan Baumann, *A Beautiful Way* (Seattle: YWAM Publishing, 2008), 99.

[2] Nettleton, *When Faith,* 129–132.

[3] Baumann, *Beautiful Way*, 93.

CHAPTER 8

[1] Thomas Aquinas, *Lutheran Service Book #640*: "Thee We Adore, O Hidden Savior." Translators: James R. Woodford, Stephen P Starke. Concordia Publishing House, 2006.

ABOUT THE VOICE OF THE MARTYRS

The Voice of the Martyrs (VOM) serves persecuted Christians in the world's most difficult and dangerous places to follow Christ, while inspiring all members of the global body of Christ to enter into fellowship with them. VOM was founded in 1967 by Pastor Richard Wurmbrand (1909–2001) and his wife, Sabina (1913–2000). Richard was imprisoned 14 years in Communist Romania for his faith in Christ, and Sabina was imprisoned for three years. Soon after their imprisonment, they founded VOM and established a family of missions dedicated to assisting persecuted Christians worldwide. Since then, VOM has been dedicated to inspiring all believers to a biblical faith by telling the stories of persecuted Christians, thereby inspiring a deeper commitment to Christ and the fulfillment of his Great Commission, no matter the cost.

To be inspired by the bold faith of our persecuted brothers and sisters in Christ who are working to advance the gospel in hostile areas and restricted nations, request a free subscription to VOM's award-winning monthly magazine. Visit us at vom.org, or call 800-747-0085.

To learn more about VOM's work, please contact us:

United States . . . . vom.org
Australia . . . . vom.com.au
Belgium . . . . hvk-aem.be
Brazil . . . . maisnomundo.org

Canada	vomcanada.com
Czech Republic	hlas-mucedniku.cz
Finland	marttyyrienaani.fi
The Netherlands	sdok.nl
New Zealand	vom.org.nz
Poland	gpch.pl
Portugal	vozdosmartires.com
Singapore	gosheninternational.org
South Africa	persecutionsa.org
South Korea	vomkorea.kr
United Kingdom	releaseinternational.org